The Car Design Yearbook 3

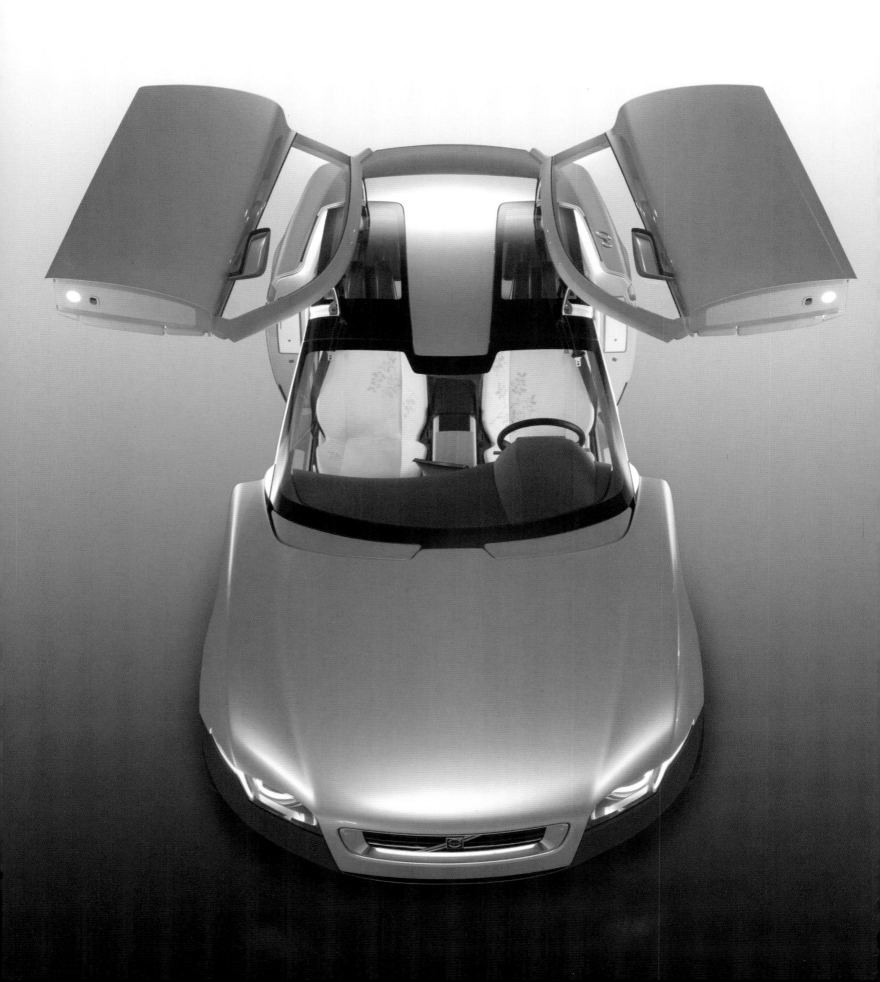

Stephen Newbury

The Car Design Yearbook

the definitive annual guide to all new
concept and production cars worldwide

MERRELL
LONDON · NEW YORK

MERRELL

First published 2004 by Merrell Publishers Limited

Head office
42 Southwark Street
London SE1 1UN
Telephone +44 (0)20 7403 2047
E-mail mail@merrellpublishers.com

New York office
49 West 24th Street
New York, NY 10010
Telephone 212 929 8344
E-mail info@merrellpublishersusa.com

www.merrellpublishers.com

Publisher Hugh Merrell
Editorial Director Julian Honer
US Director Joan Brookbank
Sales and Marketing Director Emilie Amos
Sales and Marketing Executive Emily Sanders
Managing Editor Anthea Snow
Editor Sam Wythe
Design Manager Nicola Bailey
Production Manager Michelle Draycott
Design and Production Assistant Matt Packer

British Library Cataloguing-in-Publication data:
Newbury, Stephen
The car design yearbook 3 : the definitive annual
guide to all new concept and production cars
worldwide
1.Automobiles 2.Automobiles – Design
I.Title
629.2'22

ISBN 1 85894 241 1

Consultant editor: Giles Chapman
Edited by Kirsty Seymour-Ure
Design concept by Kate Ward
Designed by Marit Münzberg
Printed and bound in China

Frontispiece: Volvo YCC
Pages 4–5: Mercedes-Benz CLS Coupé
Pages 8–9: Maserati Quattroporte

Contents

Trends, Highlights, Predictions

One year on, the third edition of *The Car Design Yearbook* begins truly to record the progression of car design across the world. Read in parallel with the first and second volumes, this third one amply demonstrates which concept cars have made the transition to the market, and how they have gone down with the most important people of all in the world of new cars – consumers. Three years might seem like an eternity, but it's really a short time between the culmination of a car designer's dreams and the praise, or panning, from pundits in the 'real' world. Such a car as the acclaimed, and now buyer-ready, Pontiac Solstice makes an excellent case in point.

The Car Design Yearbook 3 again reviews all the concept and production models unveiled in the past year. There are 126 in total, with twice as many concept as production cars. This is similar to the ratio in edition one, and can be attributed mainly to one thing: the tremendous number of concept cars that are launched at the biennial Tokyo show, in stark comparison to the relatively few production models that make their debuts in Europe or the United States. Japan, it seems, remains a fertile ground for designers, with what appears to be a restlessly interested audience of showgoers to entertain. A shame, perhaps, that so much of this effort is expended on trivial sideshows, impractical cars that will almost certainly never be built!

As in previous editions, we have reviewed the careers of three influential designers of our time: Peter Horbury, recently appointed to oversee Ford design in the United States after carving out his career at Volvo and then moving on as design head at Ford's Premier Automotive Group; Wayne Cherry, whose long and illustrious career at General Motors must be saluted despite his recent retirement; and Andrea Zagato. Zagato is a little different from the other two, a professional and passionate designer-manager who occupies the highly unusual position of upholding a revered car-design tradition stretching right the way back to 1919. His personal design output is fairly small, but the Zagato family legacy in his hands is legendary and unique.

Also included at the back of the book are two special feature articles. One considers the evolution of headlamp design and looks at the way in which technological changes are giving new opportunities to designers, while the other examines aerodynamics, a scientific discipline that is crucial to car design

Above
With Toyota investing astonishing amounts of money in Formula 1 racing, the Volta supercar concept, designed in Italy at Italdesign, could be perceived as an advantageous link between track and road – cashing in on F1's glamour is what it's all about, after all.

Opposite
Quickly productionized after a great reception as a concept two years ago, the Pontiac Solstice combines a vaguely retro aura with the latest General Motors platform-sharing technology to create a profitable sports car design.

today. Cars are aerodynamically designed to achieve maximum speed and also for acceptable fuel efficiency, and both of these areas have an important and direct bearing on style.

The very large number of models that have made their international debuts this year and, in particular, the large collection of exciting concepts launched, is proof that car manufacturers are investing more heavily in design than ever before. Their aim with these concepts is to boost their image and to prepare the ground for forthcoming models. It is important to bear in mind that the cost of creating and publicizing a concept car is really only a tiny fraction of the cost of developing a new production model. In fact, it's surprising we don't see even more concept cars from big manufacturers to test the market. Also, with a still dwindling number of players in the industry, it would be easy for consumers to get bored with new cars, seeing them as 'white goods'-style commodities and treating them much as they do washing machines and refrigerators. Take away the fantasy or ego element of driving a car – no matter what the prevailing traffic-congestion conditions – and you would be left with essentially identical products where price would be the only element of competition. Car-makers don't want that – there's no profit in it.

Indeed, the industry as a whole has been suffering deeply over the past twelve months. It is saturated from over-capacity and, as a result, aggressively competitive. In addition, since almost all the smaller car brands have been snapped up by the rampaging industry giants, there has been immense pressure on new product development teams to share platforms and components. This, of course, saves vast amounts of money thanks to economies of scale, and quickens the development time for new models. Concepts can become a reality in double-quick time so that buyers aren't left hanging about waiting impatiently for something exciting to arrive in the showroom. This speeded-up cycle of new model launches, and the general over-supply of new production cars has cost manufacturers dear, despite cross-brand investment savings. They simply cannot afford to invest in so many new models. This has had a knock-on effect for the wider car-design community: large manufacturers with enough design and engineering capacity to develop new models themselves have been making maximum use of their in-house

Above
Smart breaks new ground with the Forfour, which introduces the brand (Smart has now supplanted the Micro Compact Car, or MCC, tag as the brand itself) to the family-car market segment. Some will feel it's a pity the conventional Mitsubishi underpinnings belie the radical exterior.

Opposite
Now in its seventh incarnation, the Chevrolet Corvette remains an all-American institution, providing (relatively) affordable performance motoring for the masses in a traditionally macho package.

facilities. That's been bad news for outside, independent consultancies, both in the pure design and the design-engineering spheres, because a lack of work has seen closures and a wastage of the creative talent they have been able to offer.

One very important new development taking hold within the major car-makers right now is a system of computer-aided design tools that quicken the concept and engineering design process. When any new car is designed, it must meet certain legal criteria in such areas as occupant vision, headlamp positions and bumper heights. If this can all be combined using complex software that also takes into account other engineering considerations for such elements as energy-absorption zones for impact protection, section sizes for body stiffness, interior spaciousness and luggage volumes, plus other constraints imposed by using off-the-shelf components, then a stylist can more easily design the car within these fixed parameters. By using a digital-rendering system at the earliest stages, a lot of the engineering feasibility and packaging work is digitally computed. These systems are widely seen as the next major development in the evolution of the car-design process. They eliminate the requirement for many costly three-dimensional prototypes and, if successful, will become the holy grail in terms of slashing design-to-manufacture time – possibly to as little as eighteen months for a car based on a carried-over platform; say, for example, a replacement for the Ford Ka using the Fiesta as a basis. That would be around half today's development timescale.

With industry over-capacity in its present parlous state, one way for a brand to increase its market share is to offer additional models that compete in new sectors but that share large numbers of components with existing models so that hefty investment costs are kept to a minimum. A leading example of this over the past year has been the Smart Forfour, a new four-door family car that targets new customer territory for Smart and builds on the success of the City Coupé (now renamed Fortwo) and Roadster … yet is actually a reskinned Mitsubishi. BMW, meanwhile, has launched the production X3 that is, essentially, a closely related baby brother to the massively successful X5. It extends BMW's range downward to new customers desperate for an affordable taste of the 'premium' SUV experience.

Another way manufacturers choose to boost sales of existing models is to develop 'halo' products that help their image (even if they rarely cheer stakeholders by generating any profit – these are simply automotive flag-wavers). There have been a number of these exotic creatures shown over the last few years, but only a few of them have yet made it to production. In this year's *Car Design Yearbook* we finally feature a production version of the Mercedes-Benz SLR McLaren, and also the concepts of the Chrysler ME Four-Twelve and Audi Le Mans, which look set to pursue a similar route to corporate glory. The Mercedes is the culmination of years of painstaking work wrestling with the development needed to pro-ductionize a carbon fibre body with gullwing doors that achieves the quality levels expected of even the lowliest Mercedes-Benz. After all, this car is to retail at around £250,000 ($400,000).

In the United States, Chrysler's bold decision actually to market its ME Four-Twelve supercar sent shockwaves through the industry, while giving the company's PR department something to holler about. It really gets one over on rivals, especially General Motors, whose lumbering Cadillac division still hasn't managed to get the beautiful Cien sports car or the Sixteen cruiser off the ground. Now Volkswagen has shown the Audi Le Mans mid-engined supercar, it leaves only its Skoda subsidiary to come up with a high-performance model – Volkswagen and Seat have done it already. But these cars are notoriously hard to perfect. This year should have seen the much-vaunted introduction of the production version of the Veyron from Bugatti, another Volkswagen 'imprint', but problems with aerodynamic stability and with transferring its massive 476 kW (1001 bhp) to the ground without components tearing themselves apart have put this project at risk. The original, ridiculous performance expectations of 400 km/h (250 mph) and 1001 bhp have now been downgraded to keep the project alive. More affordable sports cars launched this year in the United States include the new Corvette, now in its sixth iteration and as popular as ever, and the Pontiac Solstice that, as mentioned, was quickly launched following its success in concept form two years ago.

Taking an overview of all the models featured in this edition, the most contemporary designs now tend to use a surface language that is generally taut, and combines sharper radii. These cars are visibly more

Above
The amazing Mercedes-Benz SLR, built by McLaren in Britain, is now a production reality after a protracted and painstaking development.

Opposite
Chrysler is going all guns blazing to launch the ME Four-Twelve, which is set to become the fastest car made in the United States. For a Chrysler it's a genuine departure, but as a supercar it's fairly generic, owing to the obvious strictures of creating a mid-engined two-seater.

'edgy', emphasizing the metal surfaces and creating greater contrast between light and shadow. Family cars, in particular, are being lifted out of the comfort zone of soft, inoffensive shapes defined a generation ago by such cars as the Volkswagen Golf MkIII and the Nissan Micra, both of 1992. Examples are the Volvo V50 and the new VW Golf, which are both now sharper than their antecedents. The Golf is the embodiment of conservative design but even it now sports headlamps that sweep up into the bonnet, embracing the latest fashions, albeit in a relatively timid way.

Not only did BMW launch the new X3, but it also relaunched the 6 Series, a model that helped fashion BMW's sporty image during the 1980s by competing formidably in European Touring Car Championship races – and luring buyers away from cars as diverse as Porsches and Jaguars. Although absent from the BMW line-up for fifteen years, it is fondly remembered and is relaunched at a time when there is a revived market for luxury coupés. Happily, from a design viewpoint, it has an individual style that imbues it with a decisive love-it/hate-it character; BMW learnt its lesson at the 'School of Bland' with the lack of interest generated by the now-forgotten 8 Series.

The Citroen C-Airlounge concept is an evolution of the C-Airdream that featured on the cover of *The Car Design Yearbook 2*, but is more spacious and therefore more practical. The new Fiat Panda was launched under the feisty marketing slogan 'Don't call me baby' and epitomizes affordable motoring from style-conscious Italy. This cheeky little hatch was awarded the European Car of the Year honour in 2004. Land Rover marked 2004 with its first-ever concept car, the Range Stormer. A stylish, high-riding coupé, the Range Stormer slakes the current thirst for overtly powerful SUVs, and the design is particularly sporty and features amazing scissor-operation doors.

The Tokyo Motor Show comes around every two years and, this year as usual, it has no shortage of strange concepts that would look at home in the TV cartoon *Wacky Races*. The show is a true festival of the motoring imagination, because it seems the Japanese are prepared really to challenge preconceptions of car design – no matter how far-fetched the results are in relation to production reality. The Toyota PM is

Top
The Range Stormer, Land Rover's first concept car, is also the sportiest model ever to carry a Land Rover badge.

Above
Volvo's new V50 estate adds a sporty and practical dimension to its smallest model range; the interior takes direct inspiration from Scandinavian furniture design.

Opposite
Bold, roomy and fun, the Fiat Panda is an honest, economical family car. It's also European Car of the Year, an accolade that embattled Fiat has exploited for all its worth.

one example; it has a tandem seating arrangement and a wheelbase that extends, depending on speed, to provide extra stability. Such cars only serve to highlight how unwilling the Japanese have often been to set the design pace with their production fare, but even this is changing.

So what of the future? First, an interesting demographic that young car designers might prefer to pretend didn't exist: there is a growing number of retired people who drive cars. This sector also has plenty of disposable cash, and this is making manufacturers wake up to the fact that they must make an effort to design cars with such people in mind. We can expect to see more models with bigger doors for easier access, higher seating positions for better posture and more commanding visibility, aids such as parking sensors, and lighter-weight controls and user interfaces that require less strength and are positioned so that they can be operated with less movement. None of us, of course, is getting any younger, and quite a lot of us, while free of grey hairs, are getting quite a lot fatter, so it isn't just senior citizens who will benefit.

There is a shift towards bigger cars; the VW Golf gets slightly bigger each time it is replaced, as do other model evolutions. Happily, this isn't down to bigger backsides; it's mainly thanks to increased crush space needed to enable new cars to pass ever more stringent crash tests and score higher impact-resistance ratings – these have become a key marketing point. Engines are much more fuel-efficient than, say, ten years ago, but only a major shift to new fuels such as hydrogen or to hybrid power will significantly reduce oil consumption. The US government under George Bush has so far failed to put pressure on car manufacturers in this respect. Indeed, it has relaxed rules that made it necessary for car-makers to produce small cars so that average fuel consumption is lowered. Plus, of course, more electronics and convenience features all ultimately eat into fuel consumption.

With industry over-capacity and manufacturers concentrating on devising niche models on common platforms, today is a time when courageous marques launching exciting new products will come out on top and squash their opposition. Such companies as General Motors and Renault/Nissan are the ones to watch because they have renowned product gurus at the very top of their organizations.

Above
The Volkswagen Concept C brings folding hard-top technology to VW for the first time, and gives a clear sneak preview of what is to come from the German marque.

Opposite top
The rapid expansion of such brands as Hummer, with its new H3T, demonstrates that the market in the United States for truly outsize cars, especially off-roaders, continues unabated – in parallel with the long decline of the full-size sedan epitomized by Lincoln and Cadillac.

Opposite bottom
Looking like something from outer space, the Toyota PM is an example of true conceptual freedom in design.

Alfa Romeo 8C Competizione

Aston Martin DB9

Audi A6

Audi Le Mans

BMW 5 Series

BMW 6 Series

BMW X3

Chevrolet Cobalt

Chevrolet Corvette

Chevrolet Nomad

Chrysler 300C

Chrysler ME Four-Twelve

Citroën C2

Citroën C-Airlounge

Daewoo Lacetti

Daihatsu ai

Daihatsu UFE-II

Dodge Sling Shot

EDAG genX

Elfin MS8

Fiat Panda

Fiat Trepiuno

Fioravanti Kite

Ford Bronco

Ford Five Hundred

Ford Freestyle

Ford Mustang

Ford Visos

Fuore BlackJag

Honda HSC

Honda IMAS

Honda Kiwami

Honda Odyssey

Honda SUT

Hummer H3T

Hyundai E3

Hyundai HCD8

Hyundai Neos-II

Infiniti QX56

Italdesign Alfa Romeo Visconti

Italdesign Toyota Alessandro Volta

Jaguar R-D6

Jeep Rescue

Jeep Treo

Joss

Kia Picanto

Kia Spectra

Lancia Fulvia Coupé

Lancia Granturismo Stilnovo

Lancia Musa

Land Rover Range Stormer

Lexus GS

Lexus LF-S and LF-X

Lincoln Aviator

Lincoln Mark X

Maserati Quattroporte

Mazda3

Mazda Ibuki

Mazda Kusabi

Mazda MX-Flexa

Mazda MX-Micro Sport

Mercedes-Benz CLS Coupé

Mercedes-Benz F500 Mind

Mercedes-Benz SLK

Mercedes-Benz SLR McLaren

Mercedes-Benz Vision GST

Mitsubishi Colt

Mitsubishi Eclipse Concept-E

Mitsubishi Grandis

Mitsubishi i

Mitsubishi Se-ro

Mitsubishi Sport Truck

Nissan Actic

Nissan Conran Cube

Nissan Dunehawk

Nissan Effis

Nissan Frontier

Nissan Fuga

Nissan Jikoo

Nissan Pathfinder

Nissan Qashqai

Nissan Redigo

Nissan Serenity

Opel/Vauxhall Astra

Opel Insignia

Opel Trixx

Peugeot 407

Peugeot 407 Elixir

Pontiac G6

Pontiac Solstice

Renault BeBop

Renault Modus

Renault Trafic Deck'up

Renault Wind

Rinspeed Splash

Rolls-Royce 100EX

Saab 9-2X

Saab 9-3 Sport-Hatch

Saturn Curve

Scion tC

Seat Altea

Seat Cupra GT

Skoda Octavia

Skoda Roomster

Smart Forfour

Subaru B9 Scrambler

Subaru Justy

Subaru Legacy and Outback

Subaru R1e

Subaru R2

Suzuki Concept S2

Suzuki Landbreeze

Suzuki Mobile Terrace

Suzuki S-Ride

Toyota Corolla Verso

Toyota CS&S

Toyota FTX

Toyota MTRC

Toyota NLSV

Toyota PM

Volkswagen Concept C

Volkswagen Concept R

Volkswagen Concept T

Volkswagen Golf

Volvo S40 and V50

Volvo YCC

A–Z of New Models

Alfa Romeo 8C Competizione

Design	Wolfgang Egger
Engine	4.2 V8
Power	298 kW (400 bhp) @ 7000 rpm
Torque	450 Nm (332 lb. ft.) @ 4500 rpm
Gearbox	6-speed manual
Installation	Front-engined/rear-wheel drive
Front suspension	Double wishbone
Rear suspension	Double wishbone
Brakes front/rear	Discs/discs
Front tyres	245/40R20
Rear tyres	275/35R20
Length	4278 mm (168.4 in.)
Wheelbase	2595 mm (102.2 in.)
Track front/rear	1610/1580 mm (63.4/62.2 in.)
Kerb weight	1500 kg (3307 lb.)
0–100 km/h (62 mph)	4.5 sec
Top speed	>300 km/h (>186 mph)

Alfa Romeo's 8C Competizione evokes the racing era of the late 1940s, in which the firm played such a huge part. The term 'Competizione' pays tribute to the 6C 2500 Competizione, a sports coupé driven by Juan Mañuel Fangio and Augusto Zanardi in the famously tough Mille Miglia road race in 1950.

Classic design references abound; the diminutive front end recalls the 33 Coupé Stradale, the work of enigmatic stylist Franco Scaglione, while the rear sports the characteristic round light clusters of the Zagato-designed Giulia TZ. At the front, the 'whiskers' and shield grille are aligned at the same height, recalling several other historic Alfa racing cars.

Powerful, muscular rear wings accentuate this forceful personality, but it does not detract in any way from the elegance of the lines; they run smoothly from the front all the way back to the light clusters set into the bumpers. With rolling, masculine forms and gently curving features, the car is absolutely void of straight lines.

There is no doubt that this is a seriously desirable car, and Alfa Romeo is one company that has never strayed far from emotive body design language, albeit here articulated in a more historic way than usual. True Alfa Romeo devotees would be thrilled to see an evolution of the 8C Competizione become the next-generation Spider, launching a decent response to the accomplished, if controversial, BMW Z4.

Aston Martin DB9

Design	Henrik Fisker
Engine	6.0 V12
Power	335 kW (450 bhp) @ 6000 rpm
Torque	570 Nm (420 lb. ft.) @ 5000 rpm
Gearbox	6-speed manual
Installation	Front-engined/rear-wheel drive
Front suspension	Double wishbone
Rear suspension	Double wishbone
Brakes front/rear	Discs/discs
Front tyres	235/40ZR19
Rear tyres	275/35ZR19
Length	4697 mm (184.9 in.)
Width	1875 mm (73.8 in.)
Height	1318 mm (51.9 in.)
Wheelbase	2740 mm (107.9 in.)
Track front/rear	1568/1562 mm (61.7/61.5 in.)
Kerb weight	1710 kg (3770 lb.)
0–100 km/h (62 mph)	4.9 sec
Top speed	300 km/h (186 mph)

Brand-new Aston Martins do not come along every year so it's a real event to be able to include such an exciting new car in *The Car Design Yearbook 3*. The new DB9 replaces Aston Martin's most successful model ever, the DB7. With more than 7000 sold since 1993, the DB7 won numerous design awards, so the DB9 launched a decade on has a hard act to follow.

Yet, in one important area, the DB9 is not such a compromised project as the DB7, which was forced to use the twenty-eight-year-old Jaguar XJ-S floorpan platform to provide cost savings for parent company Ford. That meant a cramped interior by today's standards. The DB9 throws off this shackle with its all-new construction. It uses a brand-new bonded aluminium frame, similar to that used on the more expensive Vanquish, but dedicated to the DB9.

Jaguar-based or not, the DB7 matched buyer expectations so accurately that Aston Martin has deliberately chosen only to update the design for the DB9, rather than completely revamp it. At the rear are the most noticeable changes, with new tail lamps and a resculpted profile. At the front, the grille is low and wide as before, and the long bonnet, complete with fulsome power bulges, leads up over the fast windscreen and low roof. From the side, the light picks out the gently rising waistline that runs over the rear wheels – a truly gorgeous feature.

The DB9 is offered with an extensive list of materials and colour combinations for the exterior and a roomier cabin, allowing customers to continue the Aston Martin tradition of personalizing their cars.

No doubt about it, this is one of the most desirable cars around today, both to look at and to experience, with its 6.0 litre V12 power.

Audi A6

Engine	4.2 V8 (2.4 and 3.2 V6, 2.0 in-line 4, and 2.4 and 3.0 V6 diesel, also offered)
Power	250 kW (335 bhp)
Torque	420 Nm (310 lb. ft.)
Gearbox	6-speed manual
Installation	Front-engined/all-wheel drive
Front suspension	Four-link
Rear suspension	Trapezoidal-link
Brakes front/rear	Discs/discs
Length	4920 mm (193.7 in.)
Width	1860 mm (73.2 in.)
Height	1460 mm (57.5 in.)
Wheelbase	2843 mm (111.9 in.)

Despite being an all-new car, the style of the new A6 is changed only slightly from the outgoing model, in Audi's characteristic evolutionary fashion. The proportion is low-slung with a gently rising waistline and a roof that arches like a coupé. Linear detailing on the body is made by sharp feature lines that run from the corners of the headlamps to the tail lights in a downward-pointing arc. This suggests the effect of gravity on the A6, pressing it down close to the tarmac. At the front, the chrome-rimmed grille now extends downward to its bottom lip through the bumper level, making more of a powerful, vertical feature. This is bold stuff, likely to have plenty of appeal to the American market.

Audi's design language for the A6 is all about proportion and subtlety of surfaces because this creates the impression of prestige and the appropriate balance between sportiness and comfort. For example, the contours of the waistline and the sweep of the line above the side sills give the car a forward-moving dynamic thrust, while still exuding German formality.

The headlight equipment is visible behind the clear-glass covers and features dynamic adaptive-light technology, which turns into corners as the steering wheel revolves – a marked improvement in active safety. At the rear, the low-slung rear lights wrap round to the inside and a chrome strip divides the luggage compartment lid horizontally, simultaneously creating a striking connection between the light units.

Inside, everything is grey, typical of German cars with an expensive, sober feel. The switches and instruments are clearly mounted in the tall and wide centre console, giving a luxurious and sporty feel once more. The new Audi steering wheel has a trapezoid centrepiece on the central airbag cap, which echoes the shape of the new grille.

Hard to fault, really.

Audi Le Mans

Design	Walter de' Silva
Engine	5.0 V10
Power	449 kW (602 bhp) @ 6800 rpm
Torque	750 Nm (553 lb. ft.) @ 1750–5800 rpm
Gearbox	6-speed sequential/automatic
Installation	Mid-engined/four-wheel drive
Front suspension	Double wishbone
Rear suspension	Double wishbone
Brakes front/rear	Discs/discs
Front tyres	255/30R20
Rear tyres	295/30R20
Length	4370 mm (172 in.)
Width	1900 mm (74.8 in.)
Height	1250 mm (49.2 in.)
Wheelbase	2650 mm (104.3 in.)
Kerb weight	1530 kg (3373 lb.)
0–100 km/h (62 mph)	3.7 sec
Top speed	345 km/h (214 mph) limited to 250 km/h (155 mph)

The Le Mans quattro concept study is a design and technology demonstrator from Audi, pitched at the extreme end of the motorsport arena – after all, Audi won Le Mans in 2000, 2001 and 2002.

There's a distinctly cab-forward design and a wide stance, typical of mid-engined sports cars, while there are definite similarities in proportion to the production Audi TT and the Nuvolari concept, in particular the roofline silhouette.

The structure is made from aluminium, while the outer skins use a composite of aluminium and carbon fibre. A distinctive grille is flanked to right and left by large extra air inlets, their upper ends lying flush with the quite sinister-looking LED headlights that offer dynamic cornering by varying the light beam in width and direction. The light sources are deliberately close to their transparent covers so the designers could create a tauter and more compact style.

The centre of the bonnet curves up above the line of the front wings, which spread out at the sides over the large round wheel arches. At speeds above 120 km/h (74 mph), the rear spoiler extends automatically into the slipstream, to add to the 'negative lift' generated by the aerodynamic design of the floorpan and the diffusers.

Hi-tech features include the windscreen with its hydrophobic (water-repellent) coating, an achievement apparently derived from nanotechnology; it's also claimed to be highly resistant to dirt, to reduce ultraviolet and infrared ray penetration, and to stop the interior from heating up.

Inside, the instrument panel has both analogue and digital modes. When taking the car out on to the racing circuit, the track mode displays a plan of the circuit linked with GPS, suspension settings and gear ratio. There are also switches to operate the active spoiler, the 'pit stop' function for speed-limited zones, shock absorber settings and the track mode in the display.

It may be a fanciful package but, with the TT now getting on for five years old, Audi banks on the Le Mans to capture the interest of motorsport enthusiasts until a replacement comes along.

BMW 5 Series

Design	Chris Bangle
Engine	3.0 in-line 6 (2.0 and 2.5 in-line 6, 4.4 V8, and 3.0 in-line 6 diesel, also offered)
Power	172 kW (231 bhp) @ 5900 rpm
Torque	300 Nm (221 lb. ft.) @ 3500 rpm
Gearbox	6-speed manual
Installation	Front-engined/rear-wheel drive
Front suspension	MacPherson strut
Rear suspension	Multi-link
Brakes front/rear	Discs/discs
Front tyres	225/55R16
Rear tyres	225/55R16
Length	4841 mm (190.6 in.)
Width	1847 mm (72.7 in.)
Height	1468 mm (57.8 in.)
Wheelbase	2890 mm (113.8 in.)
Track front/rear	1558/1582 mm (61.3/62.3 in.)
0–100 km/h (62 mph)	6.9 sec
Top speed	250 km/h (155 mph)
Fuel consumption	9.5 l/100 km (29.7 mpg)

The outgoing 5 Series was always going to be a very hard act to follow for BMW: it was widely regarded as the ultimate mid-sized executive saloon, and received unstinting praise from motoring pundits. But, at seven years old, it had to go sometime.

First impressions of the new 5 are of a car that has evolved with only subtle changes. New headlights, complete with 'eyebrows', sweep back along the wings, while powerful lines race across the bonnet to define a muscular shoulder and powerful-looking front end.

This is the first BMW without the traditional swage line (crease line) along its side, ending a central 5 Series tenet begun in 1972. On the new car it is replaced by a contour line that runs from the bonnet just above the headlights, all the way to the back to just above the tail lights. Reflections above and below this line, as well as low door sills and the absence of protective door strips, boost the side profile's depth considerably, so that the side view hints at a coupé form, with its raked rear screen and sweeping C-pillar that kinks on to the boot.

A whole host of new technologies are available on the new 5 Series, including Active Steering, Dynamic Stability Control, Dynamic Drive that controls suspension settings, Active Cruise Control, and Adaptive Headlights that swivel by up to 15 degrees depending on the car's steering angle, yaw rate and road speed on any particular bend. Brake Force Display enlarges the brake light area when the driver has to brake sharply and a head-up display system presents information to the driver on the windscreen directly in the line of vision.

It took some time to get used to the new 7 Series luxury saloon when it was launched, but buyers have come to appreciate it; now Chris Bangle has done it again – he's created a luxury model that those of us who aren't converted to it immediately will come to love … in time.

BMW 6 Series

Design	Chris Bangle
Engine	4.4 V8
Power	248 kW (333 bhp) @ 6100 rpm
Torque	450 Nm (332 lb. ft.) @ 3600 rpm
Gearbox	6-speed manual
Installation	Front-engined/rear-wheel drive
Front suspension	MacPherson strut
Rear suspension	Multi-link
Brakes front/rear	Discs/discs
Front tyres	245/45R18
Rear tyres	245/45R18
Length	4820 mm (189.8 in.)
Width	1855 mm (73 in.)
Height	1373 mm (54 in.)
Wheelbase	2780 mm (109.4 in.)
Kerb weight	1600 kg (3527 lb.)
0–100 km/h (62 mph)	5.6 sec
Top speed	250 km/h (155 mph) limited
Fuel consumption	11.7 l/km (24.1 mpg)

The old BMW 6 Series was an icon of the 1980s, last seen in 1989 when it was replaced by the strangely unloved 8 Series. BMW has now decided to relaunch the big, powerful coupé model name, to provide stiff competition to its arch-rival Mercedes-Benz.

This sports coupé has 'piercing' headlamps complete with 'eyebrows' that sit over both the grille and the headlamps, giving the impression of a machine that can slice easily through the air. The bonnet has sweeping curves that come from the squashed kidney-shape grille and define the power bulge. The bonnet, doors and front body structure are made of aluminium, while the front wings and boot lid are plastic. This combination gives, claims BMW, better pedestrian protection while at the same time reducing weight.

The new 6 Series benefits from BMW's quantum leap forward in interior design. When the final model of the original 6 Series vanished in 1989, BMW had ended up with a mid-1970s design that had become weighty with 1980s electronics ... which meant dozens of messy buttons and switches. Today there's even more inbuilt technology, but the neat iDrive system ensures that the controls are much more easily usable.

In fact, technology levels are similar to the new 5 Series. Dynamic Driving Control sharpens up throttle reaction for responsive acceleration and a more direct feel from the power-assisted steering; Dynamic Drive and Active Steering minimize body roll in bends by actively stiffening the rollbars; Active Cruise Control keeps the car at a pre-selected speed and monitors traffic ahead to ensure an appropriate distance is maintained; and Adaptive Headlights improve visibility by swivelling by up to 15 degrees in bends. There's also a new head-up display system.

BMW intends never to let its Stuttgart rivals outwit it again: which is why, unlike either the first 6 Series or the 8 Series, there will soon be a 'new 6' convertible model too.

BMW X3

Design	Chris Bangle
Engine	3.0 in-line 6 (2.5, and 3.0 diesel, also offered)
Power	172 kW (231 bhp) @ 5900 rpm
Torque	300 Nm (221 lb. ft.) @ 3500 rpm
Gearbox	6-speed manual
Installation	Front-engined/all-wheel drive
Front suspension	Spring strut axle
Rear suspension	Central arm axle with longitudinal arms
Brakes front/rear	Discs/discs
Front tyres	235/55R17
Rear tyres	235/55R17
Length	4565 mm (179.7 in.)
Width	1853 mm (73 in.)
Height	1674 mm (65.9 in.)
Wheelbase	2795 mm (110 in.)
Track front/rear	1524/1542mm (60/60.7 in.)
Kerb weight	1800 kg (3968 lb.)
0–100 km/h (62 mph)	7.8 sec
Top speed	209 km/h (130 mph)
Fuel consumption	11.4 l/100 km (24.8 mpg)

BMW has loftily defined the X3 as the world's first premium vehicle in its mid-size SUV class. BMW's wildly popular X5 has, to date, created the X Series 'Sports Activity Vehicle' sub-brand in its own right, so the company is sensible to exploit this by introducing a lower-cost version that many more people can afford.

The X3 uses the increasingly familiar modern BMW design language, with the interplay of concave and convex surfaces giving it its fresh appearance. There is the reinterpretation of the classic 'Hofmeister kink' (kicked-up rear-window waistline, named after Wilhelm Hofmeister, BMW's first stylist) in the rear side window and a newly designed double-kidney grille that sits at the slightly rounded front end. The roofline slowly drops to the rear to accentuate the dynamic character of this SUV. There are bulging wheel arches and a striking front end emphasizing a tough countenance.

This car is not as overtly masculine as the X5 and as a result it might appeal to more women than its larger brother. The X3 is obviously riding on a populist wave of fashionable SUVs, whatever BMW says about notionally setting itself apart from the herd: many conquest sales will surely result as it expands the sector.

Chevrolet Cobalt

Design	Phil Zak
Engine	2.4 in-line 4 (2.0 and 2.2 also offered)
Power	127 kW (170 bhp) @ 6000 rpm
Torque	231 Nm (170 lb. ft.) @ 4400 rpm
Gearbox	5-speed manual
Installation	Front-engined/front-wheel drive
Front suspension	MacPherson strut
Rear suspension	Torsion beam
Brakes front/rear	Discs/discs
Length	4580 mm (180.3 in.)
Width	1725 mm (67.9 in.)
Wheelbase	2624 mm (103.3 in.)

The Cobalt is an all-new 'premium' small car from Chevrolet that sits above the entry-level Aveo. According to Chevrolet, the Cobalt is one of ten new products joining the range throughout 2004 and 2005 and, with the Cobalt and Aveo, Chevrolet now has all the models necessary to allow it to compete energetically in the small-car segment.

Both saloon and coupé Cobalts are offered, with identical design from the A-pillar forward. The saloon has a slightly higher seating position, while the coupé takes certain styling elements from the new Corvette, and sports a tapered C-pillar leading the eye to Chevrolet's signature four round lamps at the rear.

The exterior design is similar to a Volkswagen in many ways, in that it is clean and uncluttered with a very functional image rather than using fancy, expressive styling. The body mouldings and door handles are all body-coloured, giving a clean, no-nonsense look. The deep bumpers, though, lend the car a lowered and more powerful feel. Inside, a two-tone dash with wood trim and leather gives an upmarket appearance. Gauges, knobs and buttons are all clearly labelled and laid out, so they are easy to use for even the least intuitive of drivers.

From a design viewpoint, this car is as safe as they come. But for those who are happy simply to blend in to suburban America, this completely new, American-built product is definitely the thing to go for.

Chevrolet Corvette

Design	Tom Peters
Engine	6.0 V8
Power	298 kW (400 bhp) @ 6000 rpm
Torque	543 Nm (400 lb. ft.) @ 4400 rpm
Gearbox	6-speed manual
Installation	Front-engined/rear-wheel drive
Front suspension	Short and long arm
Rear suspension	Transverse independent leaf spring
Brakes front/rear	Discs/discs
Front tyres	245/40ZR18
Rear tyres	285/35ZR19
Length	4435 mm (174.6 in.)
Width	1844 mm (72.6 in.)
Height	1246 mm (49 in.)
Wheelbase	2686 mm (105.7 in.)
Kerb weight	1451 kg (3199 lb.)
Fuel consumption	12.5 l/100 km (22.6 mpg)

Fifty-one years after the first Corvette graced American streets, the sixth version arrives complete with plenty of classic Corvette design cues gathered over the intervening period.

It is 13 cm (5 in.) shorter than the outgoing model, so looks tauter and more agile, but this new model features fixed, exposed headlamps. It is the first time since the Mk II 'Stingray' Corvette generation of 1962 that Chevrolet's roadster has not had a mechanism to conceal the lamps when not in use. The headlamps and wings resemble unnervingly narrowed eyes together with eyebrows when viewed from the front. The long bonnet is Jaguar-like, with a raised section over the hump of the engine to emphasize the power within; the resultant shadows along the bonnet create a racy arrow effect. The bonnet sweeps forward and low down to the front, where a wide, slit-like air intake is positioned below bumper level, extending outboard to incorporate the fog lamps.

The interior is sparingly executed, sporty and quite elegant, with undulating contours, leather-effect surfaces, and small metallic accents on gearstick, handbrake and door-release buttons.

The all-important overall Corvette silhouette remains, the waistline arching over the front wheel, dropping at the A-pillar and then rising again to create a powerful rear wheel arch 'haunch' before terminating in a blunt rear end. Consequently, the rear aspect is much edgier than the more moulded front, especially as the four circular tail lamps are complemented by four exhaust tailpipes. As well as looking 'fast', the Corvette has the world's fastest-reacting suspension. It uses magneto-rheological fluid in the dampers to control them electromagnetically, adjusting their characteristics more quickly than conventional systems for better ride and body control.

So, this is another evolution on the classic design that adds to the Corvette canon of sports cars. Plus, of course, this is doubtless another affordable top seller from Chevrolet.

Chevrolet Nomad

Design	Dale Brewer
Engine	2.2 in-line 4
Power	186 kW (250 bhp) @ 6200 rpm
Torque	325 Nm (240 lb. ft.) @ 4200 rpm
Gearbox	5-speed automatic
Installation	Front-engined/rear-wheel drive
Front suspension	Short and long arm
Rear suspension	Short and long arm
Brakes front/rear	Discs/discs
Front tyres	245/40R20
Rear tyres	245/40R20
Length	3950 mm (155.5 in.)
Width	1700 mm (32.4 in.)
Height	1400 mm (55.1 in.)
Wheelbase	2717 mm (107 in.)
Track front/rear	1537/1555 mm (60.5/61.2 in.)

How time flies: can it really be fifty years since the first and very slick Chevrolet Nomad concept car was unveiled at one of General Motors' near-legendary 'Motorama' travelling car shows? The answer is yes, and now here we have a fiftieth-anniversary update of that car-design relic – a design originally devised by GM's Styling Division in Detroit to show how the first Corvette could be adapted into a very sporty station-wagon. Times change, however: this Nomad was designed in the UK and constructed by Pininfarina in Italy.

It has a distinct two-box shape and a high waistline. The visual mass is placed towards the rear, accentuated by the wrap-around windscreen. The roof has a prominent crown to it that makes it appear like a cap on the relatively shallow side windows.

From the side, the appearance is of forward propulsion, yet the forward-leaning B-pillar would make access in the real world pretty awkward. Still, the tailgate is functionally excellent, splitting in the centre, with the rear roof section removable to allow carriage of bulky items. A sliding cargo floor extends over the folded tailgate so that items placed on the loadfloor can be pushed into the cargo area.

The round headlamps mounted on curved wings and the forward-sloping B-pillar evoke the essence of the 1954 concept. Chrome strips adorn the tailgate and complement the styling on the rear roof, another nod to the original. The interior is geometric, and also the most successful part of this design. A large fan-shaped central gauge cluster has a three-dimensional look thanks to an aluminium background and a luminous display. The classically large, leather-covered steering wheel and Chevrolet 'bow-tie' insignias running the length of the dashboard all echo 1950s styling. The black leather trim features blue inserts, anodized blue aluminium gauges and energizing blue lighting.

Is this just a kitsch birthday present or is it a pointer to the future? Only time will tell.

Chrysler 300C

Design	Trevor Creed
Engine	5.7 V8 (2.7 and 3.5 V6 also offered)
Power	254 kW (340 bhp) @ 5000 rpm
Torque	529 Nm (390 lb. ft.) @ 4000 rpm
Gearbox	5-speed automatic
Installation	Front-engined/rear-wheel drive
Front suspension	Short and long arm
Rear suspension	Multi-link
Brakes front/rear	Discs/discs
Front tyres	225/60R18
Rear tyres	225/60R18
Length	4999 mm (196.8 in.)
Width	1881 mm (74 in.)
Height	1483 mm (58.4 in.)
Wheelbase	3048 mm (120 in.)
Track front/rear	1600/1603 mm (63/63.1 in.)
Kerb weight	1836 kg (4048 lb.)
0–100 km/h (62 mph)	6.3 sec
Fuel consumption	13.5 l/100 km (21 mpg)

The Chrysler 300C – taken, in mere months, from near-finished concept at the New York Auto Show in 2003 to customer-ready production car by spring 2004 – is an exceptionally powerful-looking motor car, with its huge, raised bonnet, high waistline and cab-rearward poise giving it immense on-road presence. As if that weren't enough, monstrous, chromed 20 in. wheels give it even more streetscape dominance.

The 300C makes for an extremely impactful execution of the Chrysler face, a chunky criss-cross grille inspired by the V10-powered Chrysler Chronos concept car that made its debut in 1998. This new design, featuring the marque's richly old-fashioned winged emblem, is, says Chrysler, the 'master mould' for all future Chrysler vehicles. At the front, the hefty projector headlamps are set back from the hugely prominent grille, which itself takes up one-third of the frontal area. The chrome accents in the front bumper also convey a sense of in-your-face affluence.

Chrysler adopted a design principle termed the 'holistic approach' for the 300C. This demonstrates the level of consideration that goes into the design, as every line, angle and proportion must not only work together inside and out, but also provide a visual promise for the complete car, including the driving experience. So, after ingesting all this, you'd be hard-pushed to realize that the 300C's basis is really the Mercedes-Benz E-Class platform: this is the first time since the creation of DaimlerChrysler in 1999 that mainstream Chrysler and Mercedes-Benz products have been brought together in this way.

The overall form uses crisp, clean lines and taut surfaces. A good example is at the rear, where the sculpted surfaces sit largely uninterrupted while the twin protruding exhaust pipes hint at the V8 Hemi power contained under that vast expanse of bonnet.

Inside, roominess is enhanced by the upright windscreen pillars. Appealing detailing on the instruments and the use of tortoiseshell are luxury touches in what is otherwise an overwhelmingly grey, if still fairly sporty-looking, interior.

Chrysler 300C **43**

Chrysler ME Four-Twelve

Design	Trevor Creed
Engine	6.0 V12
Power	634 kW (850 bhp) @ 5750 rpm
Torque	1150 Nm (847 lb. ft.) @ 2500–4500 rpm
Gearbox	7-speed manual
Installation	Mid-engined/rear-wheel drive
Front suspension	Double wishbone
Rear suspension	Double wishbone
Brakes front/rear	Discs/discs
Front tyres	265/35ZR19
Rear tyres	335/30ZR20
Length	4542 mm (178.8 in.)
Width	1999 mm (78.7 in.)
Height	1140 mm (44.9 in.)
Kerb weight	1310 kg (2888 lb.)
0–100 km/h (62 mph)	3 sec

The most important thing to note about Chrysler's first ever mid-engined supercar design is that the US company is actually intending to put it into production. It demonstrates the styling extremes Chrysler is prepared to go to and was conceived as a follow-up to the show-stopping Dodge Tomahawk concept, a strange kind of supercar/motorbike hybrid.

All supercars are a statement of engineering prowess; with Chrysler part of DaimlerChrysler, it has some excellent technology partners to draw on, not least in AMG, which is Mercedes-Benz's own in-house performance specialist. Honed for aerodynamic performance, the ME Four-Twelve has been designed to achieve high downforce, low drag, and amazing 'cooling' performance, something that is vital for the four turbochargers.

It has an amazingly powerful presence on the road, and the mid-engined packaging gives it a highly engineered and chiselled look. Body detailing complements this, with lines running along the bonnet and a dramatic use of LEDs in the rear lamps. The body masses are constructed closely around the car's functional elements: engine, occupants, wheels, underbody aerodynamic flow shapes, upper aerodynamic flow shapes, and cooling ducts. These masses intertwine to create a final design package built up of straight lines and wind tunnel-tuned surfaces.

The ME Four-Twelve's body is constructed of carbon fibre and the interior demonstrates this ostentatiously, both to save the weight of separate trim and to symbolize the promise of ultimate performance and technology. The steering wheel-mounted controls include a Formula 1 paddle shifter for the seven-speed gearbox.

Mercedes-Benz has launched the amazing SLR this year, so Chrysler can call upon lessons learnt on that project in the development of the ME Four-Twelve to ensure that it really is a world-class production supercar.

Citroën C2

Design	Donato Coco
Engine	1.6 in-line 4 (1.1, 1.4, and 1.4 diesel, also offered)
Power	82 kW (110 bhp) @ 5750 rpm
Torque	147 Nm (108 lb. ft.) @ 4000 rpm
Gearbox	5-speed manual
Installation	Front-engined / front-wheel drive
Front suspension	MacPherson strut
Rear suspension	Trailing arm
Brakes front/rear	Discs/discs
Front tyres	195/45R16
Rear tyres	195/45R16
Length	3666 mm (144.3 in.)
Width	1659 mm (65.3 in.)
Height	1451 mm (57.1 in.)
Wheelbase	2315 mm (91.1 in.)
Track front/rear	1439/1439 mm (56.7/56.7 in.)
Kerb weight	1055 kg (2326 lb.)
0–100 km/h (62 mph)	10.9 sec
Top speed	195 km/h (121 mph)
Fuel consumption	6.3 l/100 km (44.8 mpg)
CO_2 emissions	151 g/km

The C2 replaces the massively successful, but now very ancient, Saxo as Citroën's new, tight-budget, entry-level car. There's significantly more design 'attitude' than in the Saxo, which has a lineage that can be traced right back to the Citroën AX of 1987. The overall proportion is similar to the Saxo's but the front end is more rounded, accentuated by the curved line that runs around the outer edge of the head-lamps and the clamshell bonnet.

The new attitude comes from the more bold, cutting and angular features that immediately draw the eye. These include the large wheel arches and headlamps, together with a deep front spoiler sporting circular spotlamps, all helping to generate an overtly sporty look. You could equate this edgy approach to Ford's ethos, but the interest here comes from the bold use and interplay of shapes, rather than linear intersections.

When viewed from the side, the C2 is very distinctive. This is good, an excellent design decision to dif-ferentiate it from the many other boring A-sector clones. The door glass has a rising waistline that is copied and translated on to the quarter-light glass. The lines don't 'flow' together but they add visual interest to the side view like a montage of trapezoidal shapes. At the rear, the large red lamps flank a split-folding tail-gate that separates along the bottom of the rear screen.

The C2 deserves to be a very big success for Citroën. It's the boldest step forward design-wise since the Xsara Picasso in 1998. If it can assure buyers that build quality, a lingering problem with Citroëns that affects residual values, will at least match such class leaders as the Volkswagen Lupo, then this should be a winner.

Citroën C-Airlounge

Design	Mark Lloyd
Engine	3.0 V6
Power	157 kW (210 bhp) @ 6000 rpm
Gearbox	Automatic
Installation	Front-engined/front-wheel drive
Front suspension	Hydractive
Rear suspension	Hydractive
Brakes front/rear	Discs/discs
Front tyres	245 x 720R540A Eole PAX
Rear tyres	245 x 720R540A Eole PAX
Length	4880 mm (192.1 in.)
Width	1930 mm (76 in.)
Height	1580 mm (62.2 in.)
Wheelbase	2900 mm (114.2 in.)

The beautiful Citroën C-Airlounge, with its futuristic styling, is an evolution of the C-Airdream sports car, a car so important we featured it on the jacket of *The Car Design Yearbook 2*. At the front, the characteristic V-shape of the bonnet starts at the grille and opens out to join the base of the windscreen pillars. The determined look of the front end is enhanced by the wide air intakes and clear-cut headlamps.

Citroën has taken what is often articulated as a simple shape – the monospace – and, by artful lamp design and chrome detailing, created a desirable people-carrier for the twenty-first century. It has managed to create a pumped-up form that has a rather organic and 'soft' appearance, projecting relaxation and comfort.

Inside, off-white is the dominant colour, creating a restful atmosphere that's highlighted with a red line running along the armrests, the colour of which matches the leather on the back of the middle seat. This is called the 'Pure' guise, because occupants of C-Airlounge can change the passenger compartment's appearance with light projected by means of optic fibres and video-projectors in the carpet and armrest trim. A 'Convivial' mode warms up the atmosphere with a glowing, candle-like light, while a sudden stream of light flooding into the passenger compartment represents an 'Intense' mode, boosted by doors and floor that are seemingly set ablaze in incandescent red. And there's more: the 'Romantique' setting brings touches of red to the door panels, and a 'Baroque' scene is created by an inrush of light that fills the passenger compartment.

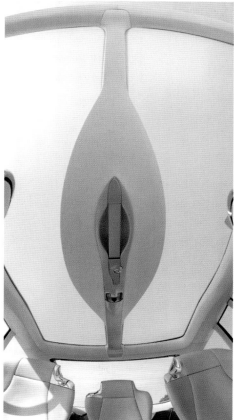

Daewoo Lacetti

Design	Italdesign
Engine	1.8 in-line 4 (1.4 and 1.6 also offered)
Gearbox	5-speed manual
Installation	Front-engined/front-wheel drive
Front suspension	MacPherson strut
Rear suspension	MacPherson strut
Brakes front/rear	Discs/discs
Length	4300 mm (169.3 in.)
Width	1700 mm (66.9 in.)
Height	1400 mm (55.1 in.)
Wheelbase	2600 mm (102.4 in.)
0–100 km/h (62 mph)	9.5 sec
Top speed	193 km/h (120 mph)
Fuel consumption	7.5 l/100 km (37.6 mpg)

Daewoo's latest is a compact hatchback designed, like many of its other recent productions, at Italdesign. On past performance from Daewoo's own largely mediocre design output (except for the Matiz), this is a wise strategy. But, to be fair, Italdesign has not excelled itself this time.

The face of the Lacetti is really dominated by the 'smiling', almond-shaped headlights that come complete with clear-glass covers and which sweep rearward into the bonnet and wings. There is a new chrome grille that tries its utmost to be bold but is actually fairly nondescript; it's the unusual headlamps that could, quite possibly, evolve into a clear distinguishing trademark of all Daewoos. Let's hope so, anyway.

The Lacetti uses a combination of tightly stretched surfaces interrupted occasionally by well-defined creases that give the bodywork an aura of strength, which is confidently echoed by the prominent wheel arches. The rear hatchback is given a backward angle and continues sloping below the rear screen to create more interior volume. At the back, the Italian use of geometric forms is most clearly visible, with the rear lamps breaking up the otherwise straight and regular surfaces. A safe ploy, then, with a mere hint of excitement. It's a pity Daewoo and Italdesign didn't feel confident enough to inject more flair into the Lacetti's overall proportions and side view, because there are promises here of a great car that's been kept firmly in check by the Korean 'Bland Police'.

Inside, the Lacetti is simple, functional and inoffensive, with aluminium detailing to give a touch of sportiness to the otherwise unremarkable cabin environment.

Daihatsu ai

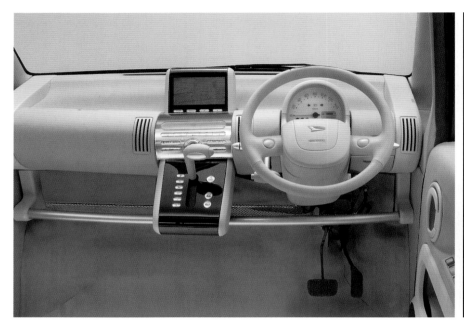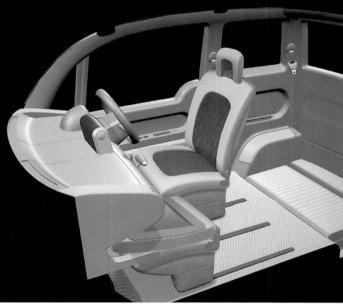

Engine	0.65 in-line 3 (0.6 in-line 2 diesel also offered)
Power	35 kW (47 bhp) @ 6400 rpm
Torque	56 Nm (41 lb. ft.) @ 4800 rpm
Gearbox	3-speed automatic
Installation	Front-engined/front-wheel drive
Front suspension	MacPherson strut
Rear suspension	Torsion beam
Brakes front/rear	Discs/drums
Front tyres	135/60R13
Rear tyres	135/60R13
Length	2650 mm (104.3 in.)
Width	1475 mm (58.1 in.)
Height	1550 mm (61 in.)
Wheelbase	1750 mm (68.9 in.)
Track front/rear	1320/1310 mm (52/51.6 in.)
Kerb weight	570 kg (1257 lb.)
Fuel consumption	3.8 l/100 km (74.3 mpg)

Another city commuter car from Daihatsu is launched, called the 'ai'. This cubic little number has a cheerful exterior, with its boxy shape comprised of simple forms and incorporating such cool touches as the sliding door on the passenger side for easier loading in tight urban corners.

Only slightly longer than the Smart City Coupé at 2.65 metres (8 ft. 8 in.), the ai has enough space for two adults with two children in the back; this is made possible because the car is front-engined, whereas the City Coupé's rear-engined layout pushes the rear floor height up. Still, those two kids would be seated extremely close to the rear hatch and so would be worryingly vulnerable in even a glancing rear-end impact.

The inside is simple and groovy, with an overall light-grey colour plus yellow detailing. Japan's crowded cities are an inspiration to microcar design and the ai has a great feel to it, much more so than many of Daihatsu's myriad other recent concepts. Assuming you could actually buy and own one, bouncing along cobbled city streets would no doubt be exhilarating in an ai. Although perhaps a bit shaken, you would emerge with a smile on your face … which is what the ai is really all about – having fun on four wheels.

Daihatsu UFE-II

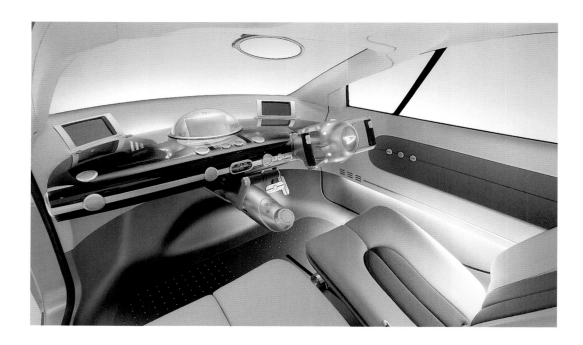

With its fantastic fuel efficiency of 60 km per litre (176 mpg), Daihatsu claims that the slippery-shaped UFE-II is the most efficient four-seater in the world. The original UFE was unveiled in 2001, and has been modified so that it now weighs a mere 570 kg (1257 lb.). This has been achieved by using composites and aluminium in its construction. The car has the stupendously low drag coefficient of 0.19 so that it can cut through the atmosphere with minimal resistance.

UFE-II appears to hug the ground with its bulbous, almost featureless, front end leading the way. As the car is designed specifically using the best principles of low drag, it is very narrow. There are no door mirrors, no exposed windscreen wipers – in fact, very little to generate any added turbulence. This is a purely aerodynamic exercise with a practical interior package thrown in, and real-world occupant safety would be poor with such a minimal amount of protection, particularly at the sides. At the rear, the body tapers in and stops abruptly, leaving a flat rear end – as advocated by aerodynamics pioneer Dr Wunibald Kamm as long ago as the 1930s. This car was designed in a similar way to a Formula 1 racing car, using aerodynamic analysis software and scale-model development in the wind tunnel to produce the ultimate shape.

The interior has been well thought through and executed, and features just the essential functions, although there is a lightweight information screen linked to body-mounted cameras.

So light a car as this is likely to suffer problems with ride and handling because the gross vehicle weight to include all four possible occupants would be such an increase over kerb weight that the suspension would struggle to cope. Active suspension could counteract this effect but this is not fitted to the UFE-II – and, of course, would just add more weight if it were. It's a tricky balance indeed.

Engine	0.66 in-line 3
Gearbox	CVT
Installation	Front-engined/front-wheel drive
Front tyres	115/65R16
Rear tyres	115/65R16
Length	3395 mm (133.7 in.)
Width	1475 mm (58.1 in.)
Height	1320 mm (52 in.)
Wheelbase	2320 mm (91.3 in.)
Kerb weight	570 kg (1257 lb.)
Fuel consumption	1.6 l/100 km (176 mpg)

Dodge Sling Shot

Design	Alan Barrington and Mike Castiglione
Engine	0.7 in-line 3
Power	75 kW (100 bhp)
Gearbox	5-speed manual
Installation	Rear-engined/rear-wheel drive
Front suspension	MacPherson strut
Rear suspension	De Dion rear axle
Brakes front/rear	Discs/discs
Front tyres	215/35R18
Rear tyres	215/35R18
Length	3592 mm (141 in.)
Width	1597 mm (62.9 in.)
Height	1251 mm (49.3 in.)
Wheelbase	2360 mm (92.9 in.)
Track front/rear	1346/1346 mm (53/53 in.)
Kerb weight	816 kg (1800 lb.)
0–100 km/h (62 mph)	10 sec
Fuel consumption	6.3 l/100 km (45 mpg)

The Sling Shot is a distinctive new entry-level sports car concept, based on the premise that such a machine must be both fun to drive and affordable to own. To achieve this, it uses the platform of the Smart Roadster as a basis.

Aesthetically, Dodge delivers on this promise. Big wheels are placed right at the corners of the car, and body lines – the rear one arching forward – accentuate their height. The look of affordability comes from nothing more complicated than a very compact size, although you can bet the company's accountants won't like that particular design aspect.

The front bumper has large inlets to draw cooling air towards the brakes and engine. There are longitudinal features in the bonnet that lead up on to the small wrap-around windscreen. The body waistline is high as a ratio of the overall vehicle height. Handles for the side doors are located above the waistline, and are finished in black to minimize the upper B-pillar visual mass while giving the lower body architecture a less interrupted look.

The upper body cocoons the driver in the manner of a true sports car. Hard-top or canvas roof modes are available: the main roof panel and cant rails are stored in the boot, while a canvas roof panel slides back and can be stowed behind the headrests. The interior design concept uses engine parts as inspiration. Hence the aluminium detailing on the piston-like gearstick, the heatshield-style trim on the steering wheel, and the machined rings that adorn the instruments.

The Sling Shot exterior is clearly dictated by the Smart Roadster architecture beneath it, while the interior would have to be softened slightly to make it through to production; it's a bit too hardcore for wide appeal as it is. Either way, the real challenge lies with Dodge to deliver the Sling Shot at an affordable price.

EDAG genX

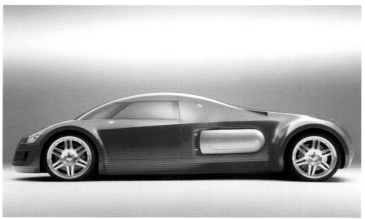 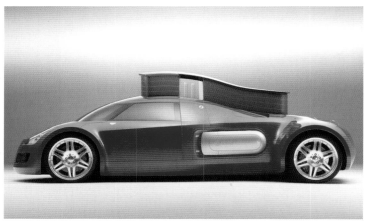

EDAG, a German-based engineering and design consultancy, launched the genX to demonstrate its innovative ideas to prospective automotive partners. It is this 'shop window' aspect that makes the annual Geneva Motor Show indispensable for car trendspotters, but don't expect to be able to buy a genX any time soon.

The genX is conceived as a sports car for the next generation, one that reflects the changes in living, working and leisure-time habits of twenty-first-century society. EDAG's research shows that the 'generation X' target group is rapidly breaking down social conventions such as fixed working hours and working locations, often working more from home or, say, at client offices. Which may all be true … but why this should translate into the need for a flexible two-seater sports car is not entirely clear. Surely a larger vehicle, something along the lines of a mobile office, would be more appropriate. But, of course, that wouldn't really catch the media limelight at Geneva.

The exterior design of the genX is very much cab-forward. With such large wheels, however, the driver environment must be very cramped indeed, especially around the pedals, for the wheels to have adequate turning clearance. The slender, tapered waist behind the doors is a major feature of the car's overall appearance, a hint at the design of Formula 1 cars, although the omission of a rear spoiler would probably lead to instability at high speed, even with underfloor aerodynamic management.

GenX has a world first too: it's the first two-seater sports car ever to feature a full-size bed for the driver! The interior is enlarged to accommodate it by means of an electronic motor-driven expander, and there are external, module-like boxes fitted in the slim waist area, which can be removed and carried as suitcases. It would seem to be an arrangement more worthy of Virgin Atlantic than the car industry, but it's novel anyway.

Design	Johannes Barckmann
Installation	Mid-engined/all-wheel drive
Front tyres	255/30R20
Rear tyres	285/30R20
Length	4466 mm (175.8 in.)
Width	1920 mm (75.6 in.)
Height	1230 mm (48.4 in.)
Wheelbase	3080 mm (121.3 in.)

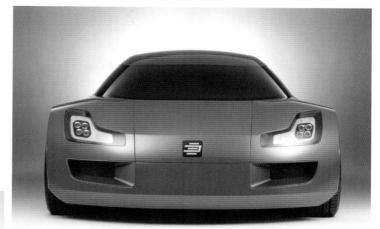

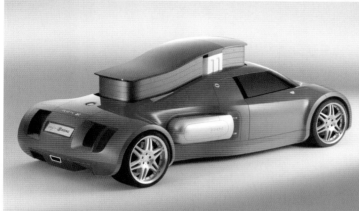

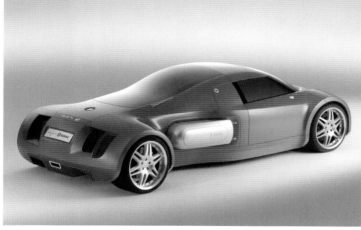

Elfin MS8

Based on the drivetrain and 5.7 litre V8 engine of Australia's proven Holden Commodore and Monaro models, the new Elfin MS8 comes in two variants. The Clubman is an updated version of the company's original 1961 track racer, while the Streamliner is a brand new and very sleek roadgoing car that was a patriotic hit when unveiled at the Melbourne Motor Show. The specification table given is for the Streamliner.

These models are aimed squarely at the weekend club race enthusiast and classic-car fanatic, and they will be hand-built to order by Elfin at its assembly plant in Victoria, Australia. Both cars are constructed around a tubular spaceframe chassis that supports the engine, suspension and bodywork, and also protects the driver. The Clubman has a cigar-shaped body proportion like the original stripped-down 1960s racer (itself not unlike the Lotus/Caterham Seven), whereas the new Streamliner has full bodywork that envelops the wheels, to reduce aerodynamic drag and increase passive safety.

The Elfin Sports Car Company has been established as a racing-car specialist for more than forty years, and has seen much success on the track with its products, winning a number of titles, including two Australian Driver's Championships, five Australian Sports Car Championships, four Australian Tourist Trophies and three Formula Ford titles. World Formula 1 champion James Hunt raced an Elfin, as did French driver Didier Pironi, while Elfins have also won the Singapore Grand Prix and, twice, the Malaysian Grand Prix.

Elfin devotees will certainly think their favoured marque is going mainstream with these two cars and, with such a great sporting heritage, it's difficult to imagine more fun on four wheels for either road or track. In car design terms, though, they are little more than a diverting sideshow.

Engine	5.7 V8
Power	245 kW (329 bhp)
Gearbox	6-speed manual
Installation	Front-engined/rear-wheel drive
Front suspension	Double wishbone
Rear suspension	Double wishbone
Brakes front/rear	Discs/discs
Front tyres	235/40R18
Rear tyres	235/40R18
Length	3500 mm (137.8 in.)
Width	1710 mm (67.3 in.)
Wheelbase	2290 mm (90.2 in.)
Track front/rear	1460/1430 mm (57.5/56.3 in.)
Kerb weight	950 kg (2094 lb.)
0–100 km/h (62 mph)	5.2 sec

Fiat Panda

Design	Humberto Rodriguez
Engine	1.2 in-line 4 (1.1, and 1.3 diesel, also offered)
Power	45 kW (60 bhp) @ 5000 rpm
Torque	102 Nm (75 lb. ft.) @ 2500 rpm
Gearbox	5-speed manual
Installation	Front-engined/front-wheel drive
Front suspension	MacPherson strut
Rear suspension	Torsion beam
Brakes front/rear	Discs/drums
Front tyres	155/80R13
Rear tyres	155/80R13
Length	3540 mm (139.4 in.)
Width	1580 mm (62.2 in.)
Height	1540 mm (60.6 in.)
Wheelbase	2299 mm (90.5 in.)
Track front/rear	1366/1357 mm (53.8/53.4 in.)
Kerb weight	860 kg (1896 lb.)
0–100 km/h (62 mph)	14 sec
Top speed	155 km/h (96 mph)
Fuel consumption	5.6 l/100 km (50.4 mpg)
CO_2 emissions	133 g/km

Launched in 1980, the original Panda was extremely successful, especially in Italy and other Mediterranean countries. It was also one of the seminal cars of Giorgetto Giugiaro's 1980s design canon. It is little wonder therefore that Fiat decided, at extremely short notice, to rename its new small car Panda following Renault's vocal concern at the similarity in the prototype's name of 'Gingo' to its own Twingo.

From the first 600 to the Nuova 500, the 126 to the first Panda, and the Cinquecento to the Seicento: all Fiat's mass-appeal city cars have had an iconic role to play for the company, as well as in the wider car industry. The new Panda was voted European Car of the Year 2004, beating the Mazda3 and Volkswagen Golf to top honours. The winner is deemed to have moved car design forward the most on a combination of styling, comfort, safety, fuel economy, driveability, performance, practicality, environmental respect and value for money, which adds up to quite an accolade for the Panda.

It is a fairly honest-looking small car, although the old Panda's 'folded paper' style has been consigned to car design history. It actually follows the proportion and clean design language of its bigger brother the Punto, and comes complete with a fully glazed upper body and, on some models, what Fiat terms a 'Skydome' sunroof.

If you're in the market for an affordable small car, this could be the one for you. The interior is cheerfully laid out and uses a combination of grey modular plastic mouldings and colourful trim. It looks playful and youthful and, just as Fiat hopes its customer base will be, is full of personality. Later on there will be a sporty 4x4 version, mainly as a 'halo product' to add coolness to the Panda brand, but also to tap into a lucrative market around the Alps for cheap cars that can tackle ice and snow.

Fiat Trepiuno

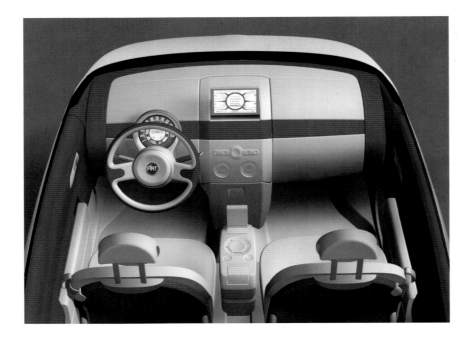

The Trepiuno concept was designed at the Fiat Style Centre in Turin to represent the theme of 'back to the future'. This fun little car uses retro design elements from the era of the 1950s and 1960s, but articulates them in a modern way. That's why it's so strongly redolent of the iconic Fiat Nuova 500, the creation of the legendary Fiat chief engineer Dante Giacosa in 1957.

The term 'Post-modern' surfaced at the end of the 1990s in relation to car design. It refers to the combining of past and future design themes, often with a playful element, and this is precisely how to describe Fiat's Trepiuno.

The car's proportions are compact and ovoid, and the front end echoes faithfully the original Fiat 500, with round headlamps and a clamshell bonnet. The roof is very arched but is made from glass that continues the windscreen contours rearward (the original 500 came with a roll-back fabric roof). This arch is emphasized when viewed from the side because of the twin cant rail lines that are made obvious from where the body colour meets the door and roof glass.

The interior is simple but not stripped bare like Giacosa's baby car, which was meant to be one step up from a Vespa scooter. The design focus is on user simplification, with a large centrally mounted dial directly behind the steering wheel and other equipment kept to a minimum. The centre console controls are under a plastic film; they are activated by brushing them with your fingers – a light then follows your movements until the function is activated. An LCD monitor extending from the same console highlights a multi-function menu.

With all the other retro-modern models out now (including the Mini, Beetle and PT Cruiser), perhaps Fiat is putting feelers out to judge the demand for a modern interpretation of its masterly classic 500. Some might say it's blown its chances unless the Trepiuno can buzz into showrooms in double-quick time.

Design	Roberto Giolito
Length	3300 mm (129.9 in.)

Fioravanti Kite

This is an extraordinary coupé that uses design showmanship and showcase technology such as LED headlamps and a revolutionary layout for the roof for its impact. A radically shaped structure gives more space for passengers in the rear, too.

The triangular roof sculpture has the windscreen-mounted rear-view mirror as its visual starting point. The shape then folds into the cabin, sweeps outward and backward, and then folds downward at the back encapsulating the rear lamps and forming the rear roof supports. The A-pillars and cant rails are blackened to heighten the new sail concept visually.

Fioravanti began its obsession with LED headlamps on the 2001 Vola prototype. For the Kite, the headlamps create a striking, dynamic feel, the apertures widening at their tops to accentuate the feeling of speed. The grille at the front takes its inspiration from Fioravanti's 'F' logo and makes a neat swoosh up on to the bonnet and along the bumper. Otherwise, this concept is deliberately uncluttered to emphasize the unusual shape. The bonnet surface is clean and there are no tedious interruptions such as windscreen wipers or door handles to ruin the look. At the rear, the lamps are positioned right out at the edges, so the tailgate opening is gapingly wide.

This sail-roofed coupé essentially plays a visual trick by converting a three-door hatchback into a coupé by way of the strong visual C-Pillar. It's something Leonardo Fioravanti perfected in his work on redesigns of the British Motor Corporation's 1100 and 1800 cars in the late 1960s. It's gratifying that such companies as Fioravanti can create concepts that demonstrate original thought – this is a valid and serious design exercise, but one that will never see serious production.

Design	Leonardo Fioravanti
Length	4444 mm (175 in.)
Width	1894 mm (74.6 in.)
Height	1330 mm (52.4 in.)
Wheelbase	2720 mm (107.1 in.)
Track front/rear	1540/1610 mm (60.6/63.4 in.)

Ford Bronco

Engine	2.0 in-line 4 turbo-diesel
Power	95 kW (128 bhp) @ 4000 rpm
Torque	331 Nm (244 lb. ft.) @ 1800 rpm
Gearbox	6-speed automatic
Installation	Front-engined/four-wheel drive
Brakes front/rear	Discs/discs
Front tyres	265/70R18
Rear tyres	265/70R18
Length	4078 mm (160.5 in.)
Width	1861 mm (73.3 in.)
Height	1790 mm (70.5 in.)
Wheelbase	2410 mm (94.9 in.)
Track front/rear	1586/1586 mm (62.4/62.4 in.)
Kerb weight	1406 kg (3100 lb.)

Ford introduced the original Bronco in August 1965 for active Americans who wanted adventure and a practical means of transport. It was, essentially, a low-cost extension of Ford's pickup line aimed at grabbing a stake in the slowly expanding leisure off-road market, where the only products on offer were Land Rovers, Jeeps and the rudimentary International Harvester Scout. Ford continued to update the original until 1977, before a much larger Bronco took over in 1978.

The upright, boxy, short-wheelbase stance, the signature round headlamps and the basic, functional interior are hallmarks of the original design that make it look engineered and at home in tough situations. The same goes for the Bronco nameplate milled into the three-bar grille. The body language uses straight lines with constant radii and flat surfaces. A winch and guide rollers are integrated into the lower facia, a clear indicator of its toughness, while exterior details include exposed door hinges, cowl vents and flared wheel arches. Loop-shaped door handles are integrated into the door panels.

A monotone colour scheme of warm silver, coupled with anodized aluminium accents, flows between the exterior and the exposed interior surfaces. The roof is made up of two separate sections, the rear one removable; roll-bar accents can then be attached to give the look of a Baja desert racer. This is another link to the original, as Ford offered customized 'Baja Broncos' in the early 1970s.

An interesting feature inside is the N_2O button. When held down, it introduces a stream of nitrous oxide into the engine's cylinders, which provides up to 50 bhp more for a three-second improvement in quarter-mile acceleration and an extra 15–25 km/h (10–15 mph) in top speed.

Ford Five Hundred

Design	J. Mays
Engine	3.0 V6
Power	149 kW (200 bhp) @ 5650 rpm
Torque	271 Nm (200 lb. ft.) @ 4500 rpm
Gearbox	CVT
Installation	Front-engined/front- or all-wheel drive
Front suspension	MacPherson strut
Rear suspension	Multi-link
Brakes front/rear	Discs/discs
Front tyres	P215/60R17
Rear tyres	P215/60R17
Length	5099 mm (200.7 in.)
Width	1873 mm (73.7 in.)
Height	1527 mm (60.1 in.)
Wheelbase	2867 mm (112.9 in.)
Track front/rear	1640/1650 mm (65.6/65 in.)
Kerb weight	1662 kg (3664 lb.)

The Five Hundred is the new flagship saloon for Ford in America. And just by looking at it briefly, you can probably tell it's not cutting-edge stuff.

Nevertheless, it is built on a notionally interesting, brand new, all-wheel-drive platform, one that Ford claims can offer some of the packaging advantages usually found only in a crossover SUV. This includes a higher 'command' seating position and an extremely large boot. The reality is that, although this may be partly true, it simply shows how the industry has gone SUV-crazy. Even cars so obviously not SUVs, like this, are being smeared with the marketing butter of the SUV. Madness; it's like giving a boring business suit a tiny sporty logo on the breast pocket.

Classic Ford design cues on the Five Hundred include the trapezoidal, diamond-pattern grille and the window graphic with chrome surround. Because the occupants sit in an elevated position, so the roofline must follow. This could make the car look tall and top-heavy yet, to be fair, Ford has made a commendable job of subtly raising the body, the waistline and the upper architecture in concert. The result is a well-proportioned saloon. The clean exterior design is understated if utterly conventional, and features gently flowing surfaces with crisp edges interrupted occasionally by fine detailing.

The interior style uses bluff rectangular and circular outlines in its construction. A T-shaped walnut trim divides up the acreage of uninspiring cream leather.

If it's practical 'American sedan' motoring with the least daring suggestion of SUV-ness you're after, look no further. If you're in search of a modern design to uplift and excite, then the Five Hundred is most definitely not for you.

Ford Freestyle

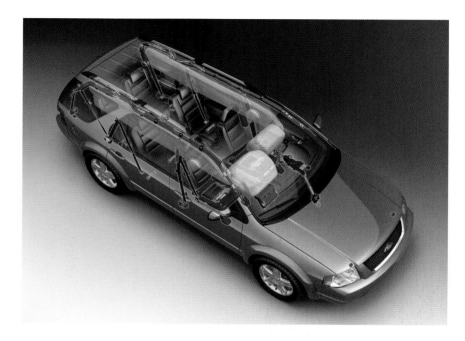

Design	George Bucher
Engine	3.0 V6
Power	149 kW (200 bhp)
Torque	271 Nm (200 lb. ft.)
Gearbox	CVT
Installation	Front-engined/all-wheel drive
Front suspension	MacPherson strut
Rear suspension	Multi-link
Brakes front/rear	Discs/discs
Front tyres	P215/60R17
Rear tyres	P215/60R17

Freestyle is a practical car for multi-generation families, no doubt about that. It comes designed as a versatile package, one that can be adapted to many different seating configurations and with masses of internal storage. It uses the Five Hundred-type 4x4 platform, but how does the Freestyle's innate practicality dictate the design and proportion?

First, there is a reasonable amount of ground clearance, making the car easier to get in and out of. The main cabin area is boxy and quite tall, so there is ample headroom. When the doors are open, the minimal intrusion of the door-window surround, due to a relatively flat glass profile, means there is easy access to and from the interior. The C-pillars are angled forward to emphasize the luggage area at the rear, which is encased in glass with a black D-pillar visually segregating this area from the cabin.

The seating position is elevated for excellent visibility, and visibility is also assisted by the large glazed upper architecture. But Ford's characteristically taut surfaces and two-dimensional lineage somehow hamper the design potential of this particular car. The overall impression is easy to sum up: it doesn't have any interesting visual details that set it apart.

Packaging is excellent, though. When Ford's ergonomists and engineers mapped out the interior, they used a 'digital buck' to determine the best positions for door handles, armrests, cupholders, and seat and window controls. They even used what they term a 'Third Age Suit', including goggles that give the dispiriting sense of the vision faced by those with cataracts, to simulate the limited mobility of elderly people. This helped define the upright seating, oversized exterior door and hatch handles, and crisp, clear instrument-panel graphics. In short, your granny will approve. Ford should be congratulated on such a thoroughly executed exercise in product research.

A little more emotion in that exterior sheet metal would not have gone amiss, nonetheless.

Ford Mustang

Design	Larry Erickson
Engine	4.6 V8 (4.0 V6 also offered)
Power	224 kW (300 bhp)
Torque	319 Nm (235 lb. ft.)
Gearbox	5-speed manual
Installation	Front-engined/rear-wheel drive
Front suspension	MacPherson strut
Rear suspension	Solid rear axle with three links and Panhard rod
Brakes front/rear	Discs/discs
Front tyres	P215/65R16
Rear tyres	P215/65R16

The Mustang is seemingly immortal. As long as the American car industry remains intact, it will always be there. Launched forty years ago, its famous galloping horse insignia is still an icon despite being attached to some cars (such as the dismal Pinto-based Mustang II of 1973) that have not always lived up to the Mustang's original promise of power and carefree style. This latest version is heavily influenced by the concept car featured in our last edition, and comes with classic design hardpoints such as the C-shaped air scoops in the bodysides, and three-element tail lamps.

The wheelbase is 15 cm (6 in.) longer than the outgoing model's, and that increases cabin space by planting the wheels closer to the extremities of the body. When viewed from the side, the cabin is positioned towards the rear, making the bonnet long and the boot deck short. The front end uses straightforwardly powerful design language: bold rectangular headlamps and large, inset, round driving lamps are sandwiched between the sharp bonnet edge and the bumper with its jaw-like vents.

Ford has been massively investing in its interiors in recent years. The cabin of the Mustang is proof positive. The cool-grey interior features aluminium bands and chrome-ringed gauges and air vents for a sporty but technical aura. The black centre console with white writing looks strong, sophisticated and uncluttered.

The exterior design of this new Mustang harks back in time for inspiration, whereas the interior is thoroughly contemporary. Mismatch or cute contrast? Perhaps the body lines will be sharpened up when it comes to reinterpreting the 1960s 'Pony car' next time round.

Ford Visos

The Visos really is something new and exciting from Ford. Although it uses many references to the European Ford house style of the late 1960s, in particular its rearward-biased proportion like the original Escort estate – albeit now much wider – and the D-shaped quarter-light window of the iconic Capri, so many years have lapsed since these models were discontinued that somehow a modern interpretation of their finer points (and there's lots to forget about Fords of that time!) seems very fresh and exciting. Still, the 'signature' fake air outlets behind the rear doors are as tacky on the Visos today as they were on the first Capri in 1969.

The Visos has large shoulders along its length, giving a feeling of strength, which emerge at the rear into horseshoe-shaped rear lamps that deliberately and cleverly highlight the feature. The centre lamp also has cameras fitted for rear visibility. The Visos headlamps are an interesting evolution. While most car designers are making headlamps a more prominent feature of front-end design, Ford's team has gone the other way here, choosing high-intensity LED technology poking through relatively tiny slots.

Probably the most exciting technological feature is what Ford calls 'Active Surfacing'. When 'Sport' mode is selected, the aerodynamic characteristics of the car change. The front splitter, rear diffuser and rear spoiler all spring into action. Active Surfacing also ensures that the integrated rear-view cameras rotate and fold away flush into the door panels when the car's locked up, protecting them from dirt or damage – vandalism, most likely.

Inside, Sport mode will automatically make the lighting brighter, reshape the seats to hug your body more closely, bring the steering wheel closer to the driver, and angle the seat into a position more like that of a sports car. At least, this is the intention.

Ford has recently produced a couple of worryingly uninspiring new models. What it needs to do is swallow a 'brave pill' and produce something as bold as the Visos to recapture the huge following and goodwill that existed for the blue oval in the 1960s and 1970s. We could even sacrifice Active Surfacing to get the drama of the Visos's basic styling.

Design	Chris Svensson
Engine	3.0 in-line 6
Power	261 kW (350 bhp)
Torque	400 Nm (295 lb. ft.)
Gearbox	6-speed manual
Installation	Front-engined/four-wheel drive
Brakes front/rear	Discs/discs
Front tyres	255/30R20
Rear tyres	255/30R20

Fuore BlackJag

Design	Erwin Himmel
Engine	7.0 V10
Power	477 kW (640 bhp)
Installation	Mid-engined/rear-wheel drive
Brakes front/rear	Discs/discs
Length	4550 mm (179.1 in.)
Width	1980 mm (78 in.)
Height	1210 mm (47.6 in.)
Kerb weight	1350 kg (2976 lb.)
0–100 km/h (62 mph)	3.8 sec
Top speed	338 km/h (210 mph)

Fuore, the independent studio founded by Erwin Himmel in 2000, is located in Barcelona and has a creative team of thirty-five. This is where BlackJag was designed, although it was built in Turin by a contractor called Modarte. BlackJag is a design study that aims to fuse the spirit of Formula 1 with the values of Jaguar, the traditional British brand. This is a marriage that Coventry-based Jaguar would be sure to approve of, after its image-getting foray into grand prix racing.

It is an evolution of the XF10, a racing-car concept designed at Fuore one year earlier, and is now presented in a more refined and sophisticated way. The BlackJag's body is simplified and smoothed out to give the car a distinctive elegance. At the same time, the arrangement of the low grille and triangular headlamps is unconventional and eye-catching.

The air intakes run more smoothly into the body and hence are more in keeping with a sculptural flow. Other changes include newly styled ergonomic wing mirrors, the omission of air intakes on the doors, and redesigned door handles. Finally, at the rear, the exhaust pipes are better integrated.

The black paintwork best emphasizes the body's dramatic surface changes, and the shapes and forms are set off by thin chrome trim that edges windscreen, door windows and air intakes.

If ever there was a cat waiting to pounce then the BlackJag is it and, with V10 power, it has very similar notional performance to the iconic Jaguar XJ220. Whether such a design-led organization as Jaguar would choose to employ Fuore as a consultant – surely the best-case scenario for the Spanish studio – in response to its homage is another matter entirely.

Honda HSC

The HSC is a mid-engined sports car that comes with some 300 bhp on tap; it is a machine that instantly rekindles interest in Honda supercars – an interest that's been slowly fading in the fourteen years since the stunning NS-X was released.

The HSC has a small cockpit that sits above the streamlined lower architecture. It's designed for function as well as aesthetics. From the side, a defined line runs up over the wheel arches and droops in the door area to emphasize further the significance of large wheels in a sports car design. The large black air intakes in the front bumper demonstrate the importance of airflow management to ventilate the engine, reduce drag, enhance aerodynamic downforce and cool the brakes.

At the rear, the engine cover is positioned high up, and forms a square edge that drops abruptly to house the rear lamps, which come complete with high-illumination LEDs to form a visibility-enhancing, three-dimensional form.

The interior complements the speed-evoking external styling, with a cocktail of curvaceous forms and racy lines. It definitely doesn't possess the upmarket ambience of a Ferrari; indeed, the two-tone blue and black trim leaves it sadly wanting in the prestige stakes. Still, a paddle-shift lever enables quick Formula 1-style gear-changing, the instruments give two sets of data information, and a CCD rear-view camera provides the driver with a more precise view of the rapidly vanishing road behind.

There is little subtlety about the HSC. Although very much like the entry-level Ferrari 360 in terms of its 'pose factor' and overtly sensuous styling, it lacks a Ferrari's well-honed and heritage-rich finesse. When the NS-X came out, however, it was praised to the heavens, and the HSC is obviously not another irrelevant design exercise. Honda could do well to productionize the car once it's got all the details absolutely spot-on.

Engine	V6
Power	224 kW (300 bhp)
Installation	Mid-engined/rear-wheel drive
Brakes front/rear	Discs/discs
Length	4250 mm (167.3 in.)
Width	1900 mm (74.8 in.)
Height	1140 mm (44.9 in.)
Wheelbase	2660 mm (104.7 in.)

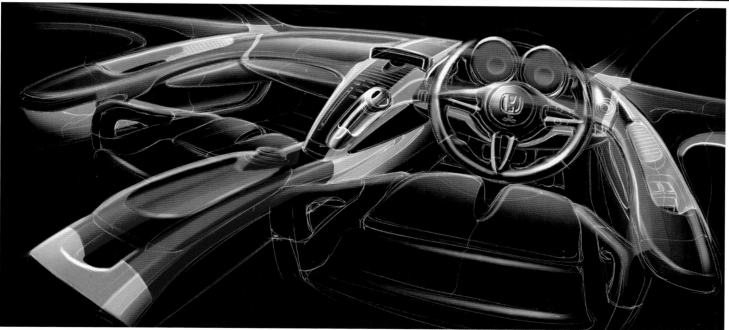

Honda IMAS

The IMAS is all about environmentally friendly motoring, and is a far cry from Honda's sporty HSC concept also featured in this edition of *The Car Design Yearbook*. Still, the radical Insight and rather more restrained Civic IMA petrol-electric hybrids have already established Honda as a leader in super-green, fuel-mean motoring.

The IMAS can proceed for an amazing 40-plus km on one litre of fuel (50 miles on half a gallon). This is possible thanks to an extraordinarily low drag coefficient of 0.20. A kerb weight of 700 kg (1543 lb.) provided by carbon fibre and aluminium body construction is also low, though by no means record-breaking.

The interior is designed with lightness in mind. It has an austere, skeletal aluminium frame that appears to be integral to the car's structure. There is an ultra-thin, transparent instrument panel and a navigation monitor that provides information, including images from a CCD camera showing what's happening to the sides and behind.

The main problem with environmentally friendly cars is that they generally look pretty awful. Right on cue, the IMAS is another pitiful example of this omnipresent dichotomy. Maybe this is because technology research concepts such as this do not get the same design attention and resources as core products intended to fit into traditional model ranges. Or perhaps there is still a spiky psychological barrier suggesting that economical cars are just not supposed to be sexy.

There are inherent design challenges that must be overcome, as the IMAS demonstrates all too clearly. The major one is how to make the overall teardrop shape work as a successful proportion, as well as how to 'lighten' the huge, lumpy rear mass created by covering the back wheels. And then, of course, there is the job of convincing the public to drive a lightweight car that is inherently more vulnerable on roads packed with heavy and intimidatingly driven SUVs and delivery trucks. The IMAS cannot help here, despite its miserly fuel thirst.

Length	4050 mm (159.4 in.)
Width	1755 mm (69.1 in.)
Height	1300 mm (51.2 in.)
Wheelbase	2400 mm (94.5 in.)
Kerb weight	700 kg (1543 lb.)
Fuel consumption	2.5 l/100 km (113 mpg)

Honda Kiwami

Kiwami is a gorgeous vision for a large contemporary saloon car. The overall square proportion is extremely striking, with simple lines only adding to the visual presence of the total shape.

At the front the wide grille and air intakes accentuate the Kiwami's width and project a calming feeling from a car that looks as if it would simply waft along. The car is set very low to the road with large wheels, suggesting that the Kiwami would be sporty too. Along the side are more edgy lines generated by the windows, while the triangular rear quarter-light appears to have been added to reduce the visual weight of the body panel and to increase light in the cabin. By doing this with such a small window, though, it looks fussy and detracts from the smooth, elegant lines at the front.

Kiwami uses a fuel-cell system mixing high-performance stack and DC motor with a hydrogen-storage system. An H-shaped layout for the control unit, ultracapacitor, fuel-cell stack, hydrogen-storage unit and other components creates a low centre of gravity, lower overall vehicle height and a low roof for equivalent headroom. This is neat thinking.

Like the exterior, the interior is devoid of unnecessary features. Extensive use of cream leather creates a very relaxing atmosphere, while the controls are inbuilt to touch-screen panels on the centre console and in the narrow display panel that stretches the width of the car above the dashboard. Honda must be ready for another stab at the luxury car market, where its Legend model went stale years ago and is now positively mouldy, and the Kiwami shows lots of new thinking for such a move.

Engine	Hydrogen fuel cell
Length	4500 mm (177.2 in.)
Width	1820 mm (71.7 in.)
Height	1250 mm (49.2 in.)
Wheelbase	2870 mm (113 in.)

Honda Odyssey

Engine	2.4 in-line 4
Power	147 kW (197 bhp)
Torque	232 Nm (171 lb. ft.)
Gearbox	5-speed automatic
Installation	Front-engined/all-wheel drive
Front suspension	Double wishbone
Rear suspension	Double wishbone
Brakes front/rear	Discs/discs
Front tyres	225/60R16
Rear tyres	225/60R16
Length	5110 mm (201.2 in.)
Width	1920 mm (75.6 in.)
Height	1740 mm (68.5 in.)
Wheelbase	3000 mm (118.1 in.)
Track front/rear	1679 /1679 mm (66.1/66.1 in.)
Kerb weight	1955 kg (4310 lb.)
Fuel consumption	12.8 l/100 km (22 mpg)

This is the third-generation Odyssey, Honda's mainstay people-carrier (the first was called the Shuttle in some European markets). It's not all that different from the previous model, although it has a new floor design that has allowed the roof to be dropped by 80 mm (3 in.), which makes it look more streamlined and sporty than usual for a car of this genre, and gives the useful benefit of allowing access to standard multi-level car parks.

The front looks wide, with its horizontal forms, and the side has a simple, clean silhouette, yet there is nothing to the Odyssey that particularly elicits surprise. This is exactly what Honda intended: it looks like nothing more remarkable than a practical, reliable and safe choice of family car.

With any new Honda, you can expect technological innovation. For the Odyssey, as well as the five-speed automatic transmission fitted to the sportier model, there is an innovative continuously variable transmission (CVT) available, which offers a fixed-ratio seven-speed mode option. There is also highway cruise control that not only controls car speed but also features radar inter-vehicle distance control and a voice-operated navigation system. The headlamps employ adaptive lighting that works in co-ordination with the steering wheel angle to change the direction of the headlight unit and illuminate the Odyssey's path when negotiating curves or turning.

Although this is a wide people-carrier, Honda has designed the driver environment in a traditional car-like manner that is intimately self-contained, rather than being 'shared' across the vehicle dashboard with the front seat passenger. This is again emphasized by the two-tone colouring used on the dashboard, which lends a very strong 'this is my space' feel to it.

Honda SUT

Honda has long been an absentee from the massive North American pickup-truck market, but that is all set to change in 2005 with the introduction of the SUT. Shown here as a concept, the SUT is a hybrid pickup truck. But it is a hybrid because it is built as a monocoque rather than in the more commonplace format of body-on-frame – in other words, it doesn't possess a separate chassis. This unibody construction allows for a fully integrated cab and load-bed. The bed is 1.5 metres (5 ft.) long and will accommodate motorcycles and quadbikes, which is handy because Honda makes these too.

There is extensive use of very angular shapes, particularly on the headlamps, bonnet and wheel arches. The C-pillar angles back along the top of the pickup section and appears like a sort of structural web. The angularity is, in fact, described by the SUT's designers as a 'billet-machined look', capturing the perceived idea of a vehicle machined from a single block of metal.

Design details that demonstrate the SUT's active and fun design philosophy include a roof complete with four-panelled skylight, a cargo bed with integrated lights and speakers, seats featuring an in-built roll-bar appearance, storage bins made from climbing rope, and front door liners with integrated Mag-Lite flashlights. It should be tough enough to satisfy the outdoorsman in every American.

The SUT's design is fairly safe overall, with just small suggestions of edginess. The engineered look is true to its pickup function, but the aluminium-covered interior could come across as a bit cold alongside what is quite a car-like exterior. It's all a far cry from Honda's traditional 'commercial' vehicles: tiny, buzzy delivery vans for such crowded cityscapes as Tokyo.

Hummer H3T

Design	Clay Dean
Engine	3.5 in-line 5
Power	261 kW (350 bhp) @ 6000 rpm
Torque	474 Nm (349 lb. ft.) @ 3600 rpm
Gearbox	4-speed automatic
Installation	Front-engined
Front suspension	Torsion beam
Rear suspension	Multi-link
Brakes front/rear	Discs/discs
Front tyres	285/65R19
Rear tyres	285/65R19
Length	4443 mm (174.9 in.)
Width	1893 mm (74.5 in.)
Height	1795 mm (70.7 in.)
Wheelbase	3012 mm (118.6 in.)
Track front/rear	1650/1664 mm (65/65.5 in.)
Kerb weight	2109 kg (4650 lb.)

The H3T is unmistakably a Hummer. It's youthful and masculine, but it's much more inclusive than the larger and more military-looking H2. This is a new, smaller product that uses the strength of the macho Hummer brand (originally derived from a military vehicle) to access a new market. It's a mid-size 'truck' that is immediately more manageable and less obese than anything seen in news reports from Iraq or Afghanistan.

New thinking here on the H3T includes side-access doors into the load bay with ingenious drop-down steps that double as weather-tight storage compartments. A power-operated folding canvas sunroof combines with the drop-down rear window to offer an open-air driving experience. The off-road potential is obvious, with huge ground clearance that gives it a 51-degree approach angle and a 50-degree departure angle, critical measurements for off-road performance. A camera mounted on the bonnet can record off-road excursions in DVD format.

An unusual partnership was born during the creation of the H3T. Hummer collaborated with sportswear masters Nike on several key aspects of the vehicle's design. The combined effort led to the creation of a new tyre designed for multiple traction environments, featuring 'sand paddles', traction pads and different tread patterns across the tyre (defined by different colours, apeing Nike's ACG trail and hiking shoes), which can cope with different surfaces.

For the interior, Nike's influence includes the use of lightweight Sphere material on the seats. Nike uses this in specialized clothing that automatically cools or warms the body. The seats also feature Nike Epic backpacks integrated into seat-back clamshells. The interior boasts military-inspired toggle switches, an altimeter, a compass and an inclinometer so that every occupant can, as they say, 'just do it'.

Hyundai E3

The E3 (pronounced "E cubed") concept is Hyundai's considered view of a mid-sized C-segment car for the future. Designed at its European Design Centre in Germany, the E3, Hyundai says, has evolved from the inside out, following the Renault approach to user-friendly interiors.

The spacious cabin uses a combination of calming pastel shades with the aim of inducing complete relaxation by reducing stress and increasing comfort. The management of light in the cabin is a key element in providing a soothing environment. Hyundai has done this by incorporating a tinted glass roof with a 'floating' opaque panel that carries courtesy lights and sun visors and also provides filtered ambient light.

For the dashboard, there is a multi-tiered centre console, and thoughtful attention has been directed to the instruments, with conventional dials and gauges replaced by a multi-function speedometer, plus a retractable LCD information screen.

The E3 has an aerodynamic side profile with a steeply rising bonnet that continues up on to the windscreen in a constant angled line. The exterior is made up of mainly rectangular elements with tightly rounded corners. This approach is too fussy at the rear, while the front end also lacks a strong identity because of it. Special two-part hinges allow the doors to be opened to 90 degrees. The E3 also boasts an electrically operated bicycle carrier integrated into the rear number plate mounting – a neat touch that consumers would adore.

Hyundai has some great ideas in the E3; only the exterior style is lacking the necessary sophistication to make this a production proposition.

Engine	1.8 in-line 4
Power	104 kW (140 bhp)
Front suspension	MacPherson strut
Rear suspension	Multi-link
Length	4150 mm (163.4 in.)
Wheelbase	2650 mm (104.3 in.)

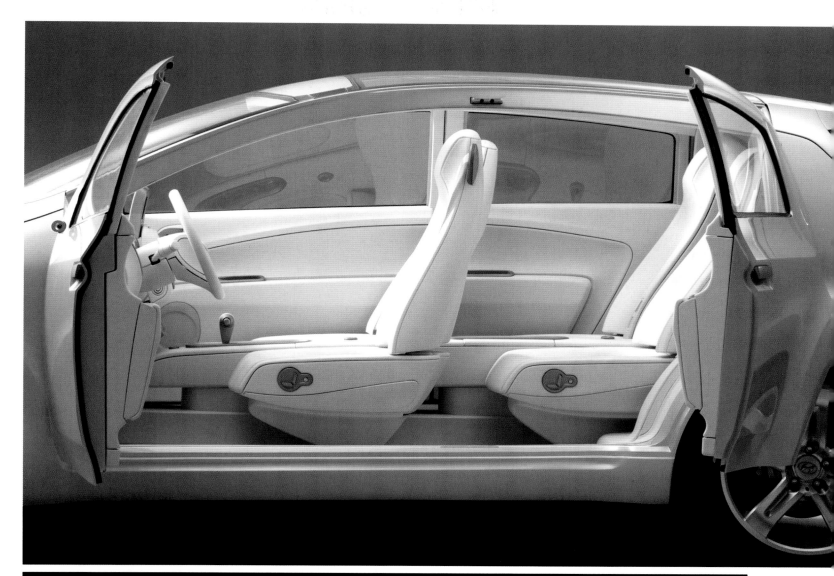

Hyundai HCD8

Design	Chris Zarlenga
Engine	2.7 V6
Gearbox	6-speed manual
Installation	Front-engined/front-wheel drive
Brakes front/rear	Discs/discs
Front tyres	255/40R19
Rear tyres	255/40R19
Length	4326 mm (170.3 in.)
Width	1822 mm (71.7 in.)
Height	1339 mm (52.7 in.)
Wheelbase	2633 mm (103.7 in.)
Track front/rear	1804/1806 mm (71/71.1 in.)

Hyundai's new supercar concept is the first car to emerge from its new Design and Technical Center in Irvine, California. Visually striking, the HCD8 mixes sharp angular features with large powerful surfaces to maximum effect. The headlamps are extremely piercing, narrowed and slanted, made possible by using LED technology; meanwhile, the grille looks like an open jaw that suggests the fangs of power lurking just behind it. The rearward-biased body proportion, and in particular the heaviness around the rear end, is similar to the Porsche 928 of the 1970s.

A high, rising waistline cocoons the occupants and gives a feeling of security, especially in the rear, where access is achieved by squeezing over the sill and around the B-pillar. Once inside, two-tone grey leather seating with wood flooring certainly looks good but could be rather slippery for climbing in and out of a close-coupled sports car like this. The other trim includes wood and nickel-aluminium on the steering wheel and gearknob. The overall effect is light and contemporary because it utilizes restful tones.

The driver can adjust the HCD8's ride height by 10 cm (4 in.) through the air suspension, so the car can sit low to the ground at high speeds when touring or can be raised up for better ground clearance when needed.

Unfortunately, though, no matter what the clever details, Hyundai does not really have the brand strength to carry off a convincing supercar design in what is a very image-conscious market. Unless, of course, it was uncommonly affordable and also superior to established marques – which is closer to home territory for the company.

Hyundai Neos-II

Brakes front/rear	Discs/discs
Front tyres	255/35ZR20
Rear tyres	255/35ZR20
Length	3835 mm (151 in.)
Width	1775 mm (69.9 in.)
Height	1585 mm (62.4 in.)

Hyundai desperately needs to redefine its image, but this model just doesn't do it from a design standpoint, despite its eye-catching livery. The concept Neos-II was designed at Hyundai's design centre in Chibahis, Japan, and is supposed to represent a possible luxurious four-seater of the near-future that also has crossover sports-utility capability.

The tall front-end design features menacing-looking headlamps that use adaptive technology, allowing them to bend their beam into corners to improve visibility. There is a large front door and a smaller sliding door at the rear that uses a multi-link system, making it easier to get in and out.

The concept car was shown in black with red accent lines that link the exterior to the interior, which is primarily covered in rich red leather with grey and aluminium detailing. The dashboard makes extensive use of touch-screen controls and digital displays. A lot of functionality is built into the centre console control panel and then projected on the small screen in the centre, making it difficult to have effortless access to information. This is just one of many aspects that lack detail consistency.

Hyundai has realized that improving the design of its products is fundamental to growth, and has expanded its design centres in Chibahis, California and Germany to work under close guidance from the central design hub in Namyang, South Korea. But for every move it takes forward, its leading Western rivals, such as Volkswagen and Peugeot, remain a step ahead both in the show-car stakes and, it has to be said, in the showroom itself. "Could do better" is perhaps the reluctant summary.

Infiniti QX56

Design	Diane Allen
Engine	5.6 V8
Power	235 kW (315 bhp) @ 4900 rpm
Torque	529 Nm (390 lb. ft.) @ 3600 rpm
Gearbox	5-speed automatic
Installation	Front-engined/all-wheel drive
Front suspension	Double wishbone
Rear suspension	Double wishbone
Brakes front/rear	Discs/discs
Front tyres	265/70R18
Rear tyres	265/70R18
Length	5255 mm (206.9 in.)
Width	2002 mm (78.8 in.)
Height	1999 mm (78.7 in.)
Wheelbase	3129 mm (123.2 in.)
Track front/rear	1715/1715 mm (67.5/67.5 in.)
Kerb weight	2554 kg (5631 lb.)
Fuel consumption	18 l/100 km (16 mpg)

Another gas-guzzling SUV that's set to grace the streets of North America in 2004. Infiniti has added the QX56 – a new, full-sized, V8-powered SUV based on the Nissan Pathfinder – to its model line-up, and named it after its 5.6 litre engine. Some will revere its nominal power, although with 'just' 315 bhp on tap, this is a unit configured for torque rather than acceleration; others will find it obscene and unnecessary.

This is a huge car that stands almost two metres tall and weighs more than 2.5 tonnes. The design is powerful and has significant on-road presence. The bonnet height is seemingly enormous, and drops suddenly down to a large, horizontally slatted chrome grille. The headlamps sit slightly lower than this, for legislative requirements but also to emphasize the taller, altar-like grille. You certainly won't miss it bearing down on you.

Viewed from the side, the cabin area is separated from the boot space. This is achieved by the A-pillar daylight opening line running up and over in an arc until it reaches the C-pillar, where it turns and angles slightly forward. By comparison, the rear quarter-light window has a horizontal top edge to differentiate this portion of the glasshouse space clearly.

The rear, indeed, looks messy in comparison with the rest of the body. The lamps are surprisingly narrow and upright, which adds to the feeling of extreme height. Lamps that crossed over on to the tailgate panel would have lowered the visual centre of gravity, but that is clearly not what Infiniti desired.

The interior has a tall centre stack and console, with high-mounted and easy-to-read controls. The two-tone colour scheme is restful and the leather-appointed seats complement the blonde Apaya-wood trim and aluminium accents.

Italdesign Alfa Romeo Visconti

When Alfa Romeo decides to link up with Giorgetto Giugiaro's Italdesign to produce a flagship sports-saloon concept, you just know the end result will be an exciting treat. Giugiaro has an association with Alfa that stretches back over his entire working life. The first production model he designed was the Alfa 2000 Sprint in 1960, when employed by Bertone and aged just twenty-two, and in 1971 his Alfasud family car was much vaunted.

Here, Giugiaro has schemed the Visconti as a two-volume car rather than as a traditional 'three-box' four-door saloon. Perhaps the most highly visible aspect of the car's design is its shapely, downward-sloping tail end. Back in 1993 Giugiaro designed the Bugatti EB 112 concept super-saloon, which has clearly been a source of inspiration for the rear treatment here, but the Alfa Brera concept, shown in 2002, is also what the Visconti has evolved from.

The Alfa Romeo grille is incorporated into the Visconti, where it has grown bolder and bigger, with fewer chrome strips, which are now thicker and more widely spaced apart from each other. There are six air intakes at the front to cool the engine and brakes, together with menacing, wide-eyed headlamps, created by using triple circular reflectors. The Visconti's short, smooth and compact frontal treatment is not just about sportiness. If this is indeed the style of the next 166, as Alfa Romeo wants us to believe, then such proportions are needed to comply with new EU pedestrian impact standards due to come into force in 2005; these call for more vertical fronts, with bonnet lines raised well above engine level, to cushion unlucky accident victims, and they will apply to all new cars launched in the territory from then on. Enthusiasts may deplore the move but, for designers, it's yet another legislative challenge to be overcome – the very stuff of modern car design.

The shaping of the low, muscular and cut-off tail end reflects a car designed for style rather than BMW-esque sensibleness, and is sure to end up on the 'cutting-room floor', so to speak. Otherwise, assuming the Italian manufacturer is brave enough to build it, such a model as this would take Alfa Romeo up a notch in the prestige stakes.

Design	Italdesign
Engine	3.2 V6
Power	302 kW (405 bhp) @ 6000 rpm
Installation	Front-engined/rear-wheel drive
Length	4955 mm (195.1 in.)
Width	1896 mm (74.6 in.)
Height	1474 mm (58 in.)
Wheelbase	2825 mm (111.2 in.)
Track front/rear	1595/1615 mm (62.8/63.6 in.)

Italdesign Toyota Alessandro Volta

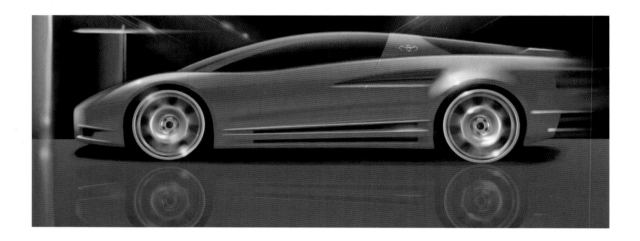

Design	Italdesign
Engine	Twin electric motors and 3.3 V6
Power	304 kW (408 bhp)
Installation	Front- and rear-mounted/all-wheel drive
Front suspension	Double wishbone
Rear suspension	Double wishbone
Brakes front/rear	Discs/discs
Front tyres	245/40ZR19
Rear tyres	285/40ZR19
Length	4358 mm (171.6 in.)
Width	1925 mm (75.8 in.)
Height	1140 mm (44.9 in.)
Wheelbase	2570 mm (101.2 in.)
Track front/rear	1652/1640 mm (65/64.6 in.)
Kerb weight	1250 kg (2756 lb.)
0–100 km/h (62 mph)	4.3 sec
Top speed	250 km/h (155 mph)

Italdesign and Toyota have come together to design the Alessandro Volta, a hybrid-powered coupé with classic mid-engined supercar proportions.

The hybrid powertrain is mounted centrally, just behind the cockpit, to power the rear wheels, while the front wheels get their motivation from a second electric motor. There is a V6 petrol engine mounted behind the rear axle for when it's needed. This set-up gives all-wheel-drive propulsion all of the time and, because of the flat floor arrangement, seating for three is possible.

The front air intake creates a dramatic first impression. The front end curves in plan view from the edges of the intake around and below the slanting headlamps to the wheel arches. The bonnet line is very low and rises straight to the windscreen. At the rear, the tail abruptly truncates; at the base of the rear screen is a spoiler for creating downforce, and below the flat rear panel are a series of multiple outlets for expelling hot air from the rear-mounted engine. The doors are termed 'dragonfly-wing' and hinge upward. In the body side, a sturdy beltline stretches upward over the rear wheel arch, creating two characterful 'claw-marks' at the back of the doors.

Drive-by-wire technology and floor rails combine to allow the driver's seat, pedals and steering wheel to slide to the right or left for the perfect command position.

The Volta is a highly dramatic creation by Italdesign. Quite why Toyota needs a supercar concept like this is unclear, although a marketing department the size of Toyota's no doubt has its reasons. Undoubtedly, the Volta provides a sexier showcase for the firm's acclaimed hybrid technology than the more mundane Prius saloon. And Toyota, as we know, is an organization that likes to have every base covered.

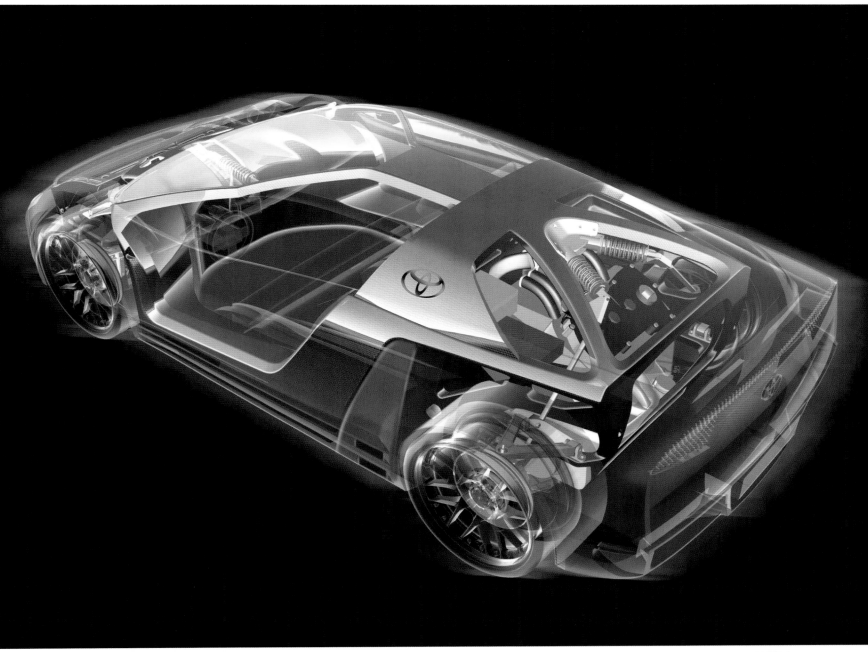

Italdesign Toyota Alessandro Volta **103**

Jaguar R-D6

Design	Ian Callum
Engine	2.7 V6 diesel
Power	172 kW (230 bhp)
Torque	500 Nm (368 lb. ft.)
Gearbox	6-speed manual
Installation	Front-engined/four-wheel drive
Brakes front/rear	Discs/discs
Front tyres	255/30R21
Rear tyres	275/30R21
Length	4330 mm (170.5 in.)
Width	2150 mm (84.6 in.)
Height	1390 mm (54.7 in.)
Wheelbase	2840 mm (111.8 in.)
Kerb weight	1500 kg (3307 lb.)
0–100 km/h (62 mph)	< 6 sec
Top speed	250 km/h (155 mph) limited

Evolving from the Jaguar R-Coupé concept launched a year earlier, the R-D6 is a bang-up-to-date sports saloon complete with the emotive surfaces that should come with every Jaguar. Here is a compact saloon but with decidedly un-Jaguar-like small overhangs and very short rear doors. The roofline extends a long way rearward to give adequate headroom to rear occupants; the C-pillars wrap inward, creating a sculpted shoulder over the rear wings, and continue to the rear and the oval screen. This is a rear design quite unlike anything we've seen before on a Jaguar.

The depth of design detail shows the importance with which Jaguar rates this concept. The lamps use LED technology front and rear; the side-hinged tailgate gives more rear headroom and mimics the iconic 1961 E-type coupé. Flush-mounted door handles pivot on their front edges to activate electrical actuators that open the door.

Inside, Jaguar has used the familiar leather and wood in new ways: carbon-black aniline leather and thick, black saddle leather complement the satin-finish, black American-walnut veneer that runs from the front to the rear of the cabin. Your feet actually rest on wood, which again runs from front to rear. The leatherwork appears from some angles to be like a floating structure in the cabin.

Another satisfying touch is the silver starter button, located in the top of the gearshift below a swivelling top piece like the safety-catch on a gun or the top of a fighter-aircraft joystick.

Jeep Rescue

Design	Mark Allen, John Sgalia and Dan Zimmermann
Engine	5.9 V8 turbo-diesel
Power	242 kW (325 bhp)
Torque	814 Nm (600 lb. ft.)
Gearbox	6-speed manual
Installation	Front-engined/four-wheel drive
Front suspension	Solid live axle
Rear suspension	Heavy-duty link-coil
Brakes front/rear	Discs/discs
Front tyres	315/80R18
Rear tyres	315/80R18
Length	4907 mm (193.2 in.)
Width	2062 mm (81.2 in.)
Height	2139 mm (84.2 in.)
Wheelbase	3106 mm (122.3 in.)
Kerb weight	2722 kg (6000 lb.)

Given the popularity of the Hummer H2, the Jeep Design Studio in Detroit set out to create what it describes as the 'ultimate execution' of a Jeep. Hence the Rescue, a trail search-and-rescue vehicle geared towards the likes of firefighters, gamekeepers, park rangers and ski resort personnel. It comes with all the Jeep DNA that you could possibly expect; it's like an outsize Wrangler, in fact. The ground clearance is huge, with the lower body using grey-coloured parts, to protect the painted upper body from damage when off-road.

With seating for five, its primary mission is its emergency capability. It comes with an impressive array of rescue equipment that includes a 10 kW power generator, 3D topographical mapping software and navigation system, under-chassis cameras for avoiding obstructions when winching by remote control, infra-red thermal cameras for finding lost people, a satellite telephone, a VHF radio, a digital video recorder with satellite transmission, and exterior perimeter illumination with specific lighting for long-distance searches.

But the Rescue isn't all about serious endeavours. It comes with removable doors and a folding windscreen that make it a fun adventure vehicle too: it can be configured to run almost totally open, with a retractable back window, a sliding glass sunroof in front, and a fold-forward canvas roof in the rear.

Should a production version follow, it will be sure to start a leadership battle between Jeep and Hummer to make the toughest – and toughest-looking – machines in the car world. You might wonder what Land Rover and Toyota have got to say on such matters.

Jeep Treo

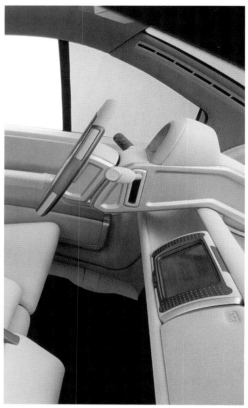

DaimlerChrysler has reassessed its well-loved Jeep brand and created something new and rather exciting here: a small Jeep. It's called the Treo and has arrived in a concept form that combines environmentally friendly technology in an activity vehicle targeting young people. Surely this is a winning formula.

The Treo takes classic Jeep design themes but reiterates them in new ways. Examples of this are the very recognizable seven-bar grille, prominent windscreen, and inside space for three people to sit across a compact cabin, as GIs do in people's imagination. The functional look remains intrinsic to the design language, right from the inset headlamps and fold-down towing eyes to the thin, motorbike-inspired mudguards.

The Treo could well appeal to the urban youth who want some light off-road jaunts in their spare time – like bouncing across the beach. The car certainly evokes a sense of fun and purposefulness with its exposed suspension and rugged tyres. In plan view, the Treo tapers to a near-teardrop shape, with two high-mounted spar wings that house rear lamps and serve as carriage mounting points for the Jeep Rubicon mountain bikes included in this well-planned lifestyle package.

Inside, the design uses big block surfaces with simple radii to create a no-nonsense look. A light and airy feeling is created by the large windscreen, the see-through front grille and a glass roof that extends over the rear cargo space.

For this target market, cost is a major consideration, but perhaps Jeep really can make the Treo thinking work at an affordable price, as Suzuki does. It's a sound strategy to get young new buyers excited about a brand so that they unquestioningly graduate to bigger, more traditional Jeeps as they get older, richer and more conservative.

Design	Trevor Creed
Engine	Hydrogen fuel cell
Installation	Four-wheel drive
Front tyres	185/65R19
Rear tyres	185/65R19
Length	3235 mm (127.4 in.)
Width	1680 mm (66.1 in.)
Height	1585 mm (62.4 in.)
Wheelbase	2450 mm (96.5 in.)
Track front/rear	1499/1499 mm (59/59 in.)
Kerb weight	816 kg (1799 lb.)

Joss

Design	Matt Thomas
Engine	6.8 V8
Power	373 kW (500 bhp) @ 5750 rpm
Torque	650 Nm (479 lb. ft.) @ 2800 rpm
Gearbox	5-speed manual
Installation	Mid-engined/rear-wheel drive
Front suspension	Double wishbone
Rear suspension	Double wishbone
Brakes front/rear	Discs/discs
Front tyres	245/35ZR18
Rear tyres	335/35ZR18
Length	4150 mm (163.4 in.)
Width	1860 mm (73.2 in.)
Height	1050 mm (41.3 in.)
Wheelbase	2560 mm (100.8 in.)
Kerb weight	940 kg (2072 lb.)
0–100 km/h (62 mph)	3.7 sec
Top speed	320 km/h (199 mph) estimated

Matt Thomas is an Australian with a dream. A thirty-three-year-old who, after graduating in industrial design in 1994, headed over to the UK to begin a career as a model-maker in aerodynamics for Formula 1 teams. After four years he went back to Australia and began planning his Joss supercar. It then took him six years to turn a sketch into a running show car.

Launched at the Melbourne Motor Show, Joss is a formidable concept. It's a two-seater powered by a 6.8 litre V8 engine and, of course, has advanced F1-inspired aerodynamics that manage the airflow both over and under the car for maximum downforce effect. The doors have vortex generators incorporated into their lower edges to increase downforce, and tiny camera rear-view mirrors to minimize drag. The composite body is built up using carbon fibre, Kevlar, glass-reinforced plastic and honeycomb steel. The spaceframe chassis is constructed of composite aluminium and honeycomb steel.

The design of such a supercar as this is dictated mostly by functionality so, not surprisingly, Matt has ended up with something that looks pretty similar to the McLaren F1 and Jaguar XJR-15 genre, with the telltale cab-forward proportion those ultra-high-performance cars boast.

Joss is actually Australia's first supercar and Joss Developments does intend to make a limited production run of approximately twenty-five cars per year. Forget designing the car – this will be Matt Thomas's toughest challenge, because the Joss will need to attain quality standards equal to Ferrari and McLaren for this unheard-of car to cut it with its awesome peers. With luck, *The Car Design Yearbook* will be able to feature the production version within six more years.

Kia Picanto

Design	Kang Lee
Engine	1.1 in-line 4 (1.0 also offered)
Power	48 kW (64 bhp) @ 5500 rpm
Torque	96 Nm (71 lb. ft.) @ 4000 rpm
Gearbox	5-speed manual
Installation	Front-engined/front-wheel drive
Front suspension	MacPherson strut
Rear suspension	Beam axle
Brakes front/rear	Discs/discs
Front tyres	175/50R15
Rear tyres	175/50R15
Length	3495 mm (137.6 in.)
Width	1595 mm (62.8 in.)
Height	1480 mm (58.2 in.)
Wheelbase	2370 mm (93.3 in.)
Track front/rear	1400/1385 mm (55.1/54.5 in.)
Kerb weight	852 kg (1878 lb.)
0–100 km/h (62 mph)	15.8 sec
Top speed	152 km/h (95 mph)
Fuel consumption	5 l/100 km (56.5 mpg)
CO$_2$ emissions	130 g/km

The Kia Picanto is a new entry-level model that, according to Kia's European strategy, will be a compelling purchase for the young style-conscious consumer. This may be true only for those on a very tight budget, because the Picanto is no Fiat Punto or Renault Clio in design terms.

Designed to fit squarely in the A-segment – the territory of the Ford Ka, Daewoo Matiz and Citroën C2 – the Picanto tries its utmost to emulate leading European cars, unlike the hideous old Kia Pride, the low-rent city car that launched Kia in 1991. The designers have done this by giving the car (fairly) sporty lines, a gently rising waistline and a quite well-executed and dynamic rear end. The front-end design lets it down, though. It's toy-like, with an over-fussy grille combined with a bumper that has simple linear features. Body-coloured door handles fit flush with the side of the car for a more 'upscale' appeal.

Inside the Picanto, two-tone fabric breaks up the interior design. There are arched surfaces and contoured edges to reflect the exterior imagery. Small cars today are gradually implementing a whole range of safety features and functionality previously reserved for larger models. The Picanto is participating in this trend by, for instance, including the option of a keyless entry system.

The Kia brand, chaperoned by Hyundai, is not the strongest by a very long way. However, if it can balance affordability with reasonable quality then this little number could sell quite well.

Kia Spectra

Engine	1.8 in-line 4
Power	92 kW (124 bhp) @ 6000 rpm
Torque	161 Nm (119 lb. ft.) @ 4900 rpm
Gearbox	5-speed manual
Installation	Front-engined/front-wheel drive
Front suspension	MacPherson strut
Rear suspension	Multi-link
Brakes front/rear	Discs/drums

The Kia Spectra is a value-driven compact that comes as either a four-door saloon or a five-door hatch-back. *The Car Design Yearbook* aims to credit especially exciting or ground-breaking concepts and beautifully resolved production cars. We cannot, in all honesty, do that here.

The Kia Spectra will never stand out. It's bland and unassuming, and made more so by the contemporary trend for MPV and SUV design influences to filter through to even the most basic of private transport vehicles. Nevertheless, designing a car for low cost is just as much of a challenge, if not more of one, as choosing the most sumptuous fabrics for a new Rolls-Royce.

The Kia has a low waistline and bonnet surface that hugs the engine and ensures excellent visibility. A sharp feature line originates behind the headlamps and runs backward through the door handles and on to the rear wing panel. Without this detail, the Spectra would look heavy and static. Designing for low cost on high-volume cars is done by keeping part sizes as small as possible and by avoiding complex shapes that require complicated and expensive tooling. Examples of this on the Spectra are the small wheels and sill sections, and the regular-shaped headlamps, doors and door mirrors. Combine all these design decisions with a Far East supply and manufacturing base and the result is low prices all round. The interior, however, is the customer interface where the approach wears thinnest; the Spectra's innate cheapness shows in the simple plastic mouldings, flimsy materials and relatively coarse finish.

Not everyone can afford, or even wants, to drive the latest Porsche or largest SUV; there is an equally valid statement to be made about one's personality, ethics and needs in driving the Kia Spectra. But it's still a design non-starter.

Lancia Fulvia Coupé

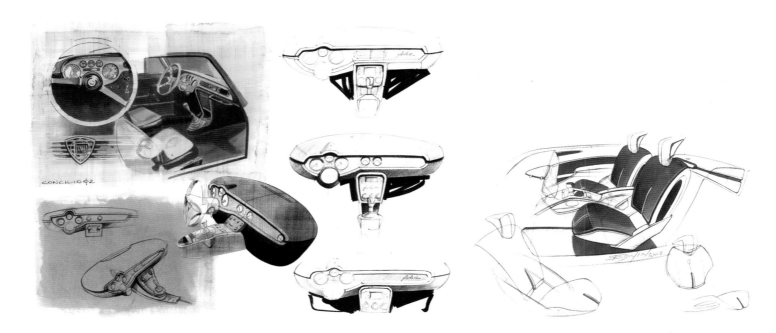

Design	Flavio Manzoni
Engine	1.8 in-line 4
Power	77 kW (103 bhp) @ 6400 rpm
Installation	Front-engined/front-wheel drive
Front suspension	MacPherson strut
Rear suspension	Longitudinal arms
Brakes front/rear	Discs/discs
Kerb weight	990 kg (2183 lb.)
0–100 km/h (62 mph)	8.6 sec
Top speed	213 km/h (132 mph)
Fuel consumption	7.3 l/100 km (38.7 mpg)

Forty years after the debut of the very first front-wheel-drive Fulvia saloon, Lancia has built a prototype to celebrate one of the derivative models that made it famous throughout the world. In 1965 Lancia introduced the Fulvia Coupé and, owing to its beautiful simplicity, had an instant classic on its hands. It took only a few touches to transform the road car into a formidable rally machine.

The designers' apparently straightforward aim here was to re-create the Fulvia Coupé as though it had developed without interruption (in reality, Fiat bought Lancia in 1969 and dropped the Fulvia Coupé without replacing it in 1976). They set about reworking the original concept and styling cues to achieve a fresh new design, and have done a textbook job that Lancia aficionados would recognize. There is a sense of purpose about the car that comes from the differential size of the strong lower body to the upper 'glasshouse' architecture that tightly encircles the occupants. The long bonnet is another proportion faithfully carried across from the original.

The visual weight of the car is concentrated over the front wheel, highlighting its front-wheel drive and front-mounted engine: the car appears to be pulled along from this point of tension. The effect is enhanced by the teardrop-shape of the car from above, with the greatest width at the front and a tendency to taper off towards the truncated tail.

Lines flow from the bonnet to the bumpers and gather around the lower outlet where four floating quadrangular cylinders recall the four air intakes of the later 1970s models. The clean side profile, with its sturdy shoulder, uses a succession of concave and convex surfaces. The headlamps overhang from the wing-shaped profile while the rear uses beautiful Italian shape combinations around the rear lamps and mixes curved and flat forms to give space for a bold display of the badge.

The interior looks back to the 1970s. The central facia insert and tunnel are covered with silky Tanganika Frisé wood that has an almost metallic sheen.

Lancia Fulvia Coupé **117**

Lancia Granturismo Stilnovo

Fiat's problematic Lancia subsidiary is fighting to keep its august brand alive and relevant with new concept cars this year. This one, the stylistic Granturismo Stilnovo, is essentially a testbed for what it hopes will be the styling cues of future mainstream Lancias.

The most prominent feature of this two-door coupé is its structural arch. This begins at the base of the well-forward A-pillar, soars along the roofline, and culminates in a low rear header position, defining a wide expanse of glass over the roof. The rear quarter-window is linked to the rear screen via a narrow channel that visually lightens and lengthens the car.

The front-end design is relatively successful, although the widespread use of rounded-off details lacks the aggressive sportiness of the otherwise dynamic overall proportions. The lines emanating from the front effectively converge at the rear, making for a stark contrast in the design of the front and rear lamps, and adding interest. But mediocre detailing, such as the back of the door mirrors, is an indication that Lancia hasn't really spent enough time on every aspect.

The Stilnovo features prominent and sturdy front wings, hi-tech headlights and tall tail lights, all apparently part of the new Lancia style. At the rear, the typical Lancia curves can be seen as defining the shape of the rear lamps, which are then 'read across' into the profile of the rear-window glass.

Here's the rub: Lancia, unfortunately, just doesn't deliver a big enough 'wow factor' in the Stilnovo. With a brand struggling for attention as Lancia's is, this new concept would have to be very affordable to steal a credible share of the real-life sector.

Design	Flavio Manzoni
Length	4236 mm (166.8 in.)
Width	1828 mm (72 in.)
Height	1465 mm (57.7 in.)

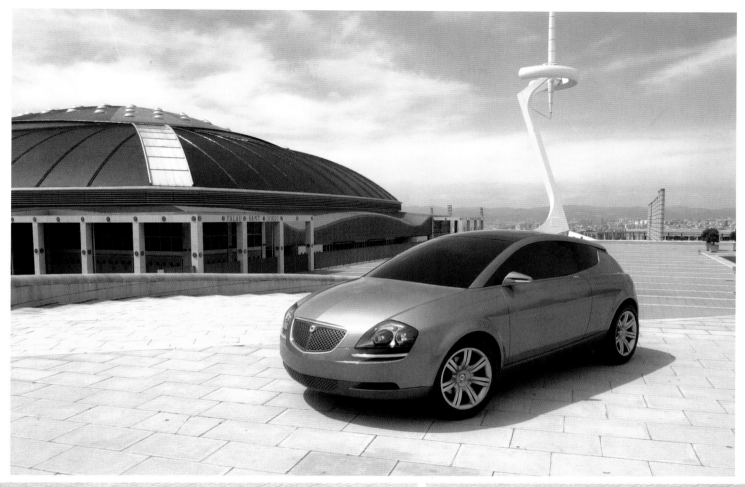

Lancia Musa

Engine	1.9 in-line 4 (1.3 and 1.4 also offered)
Installation	Front-engined/front-wheel drive
Brakes front/rear	Discs/discs
Length	4000 mm (157.4 in.)
Width	1700 mm (66.9 in.)
Height	1660 mm (65.4 in.)

Lancia has gone to great pains to imbue its new compact MPV with a warm, welcoming and refined atmosphere, and the bald facts mean it needs to do something deliberately different, because the Musa is, effectively, a version of Fiat's Idea.

Lancia has therefore made extensive use of the experience of outside consultancies to create its product. The Musa was adapted from the Idea by Turin-based creative group 515, while the Musa logo, like that of the Ypsilon, was developed by Carré Noir Italia, a leading Italian packaging-design agency. In this graphical presentation of the Musa name, the letter M apparently recalls a chaise longue, taken as a symbol of comfort and well-being.

The front-end design is an intricate one, with large headlamps, slatted grille and, below the bumper, multiple slatted air intakes. It has the same grille and fingernail-shaped headlamps as the smaller Ypsilon model but obviously the proportion is taller.

So how does the finished Musa stand up against its design brief? It isn't particularly energy-efficient and the interior ambience is a strange mix of warm beige and harsh black, with white and aluminium trim. The Skydome sunroof certainly gives the interior plenty of light but, overall, this is not the warm and welcoming car it purports to be. Lancia unfortunately seems to have lost its way in its ability to carve out a strong, unique brand identity for itself; or maybe the mainstream competition has just become far more accomplished at that itself.

Land Rover Range Stormer

Almost unbelievable, but true: the Range Stormer is Land Rover's first ever concept show car (as long as you forget the futuristic vehicles it built for the Judge Dredd movie in 1995, and most people have done). This sports-tourer targets the booming high-performance SUV segment, and showcases what will probably be the future design direction for Land Rover.

The Range Stormer is the sportiest-looking vehicle ever to wear a Land Rover badge. It uses classic Land Rover design language, such as the castellated clamshell bonnet, 'floating roof' styling, a horizontal waistline and short front overhangs. Compared to other Land Rovers, it looks much more muscular and edgy. This comes mainly from the increased windscreen rake, lower roof, the coupé-ish body architecture and various aluminium accents below the waistline. The doors are electrically powered and split horizontally low down; the upper part hinges up and forward, while the lower section drops to provide a step into the cabin.

The cabin is very simple and modern with clear lineage to the structural lines of the Range Rover, although it is considerably more intimate. The dash and centre console flow around the occupants, and mix aluminium with leather. The fuel gauge is especially novel: instead of a needle, a level of liquid drops as the fuel tank empties.

Land Rover's chassis design is world-class and a special 'terrain response' system has been developed for the Range Stormer. The car's electronics select the best programme to conquer the appropriate terrain. This entails adjusting and balancing the engine mapping, gearbox, air suspension for ride height and firmness, differential settings, dynamic stability control, hill descent control and the brakes with electronic force distribution. Luckily, this all happens automatically!

Something along the lines of the Range Stormer looks a near-certainty as Land Rover seeks to expand the Range Rover appeal to lower price levels. The complex doors, however, seem destined to remain as merely motor-show theatre.

Design	Geoff Upex
Engine	V8
Gearbox	6-speed automatic
Installation	Front-engined/four-wheel drive
Brakes front/rear	Discs/discs
Front tyres	265/45R22
Rear tyres	265/45R22
Length	4725 mm (186 in.)
Width	1943 mm (76.5 in.)
Height	1713 mm (67.4 in.)
Wheelbase	2745 mm (108 in.)
Track front/rear	1644/1644 mm (64.7/64.7 in.)

Lexus GS

Engine	4.3 V8 (3.0 V6 also offered)
Power	224 kW (300 bhp)
Torque	441 Nm (325 lb. ft.)
Gearbox	6-speed automatic
Installation	Front-engined/all-wheel drive
Front suspension	MacPherson strut
Rear suspension	Multi-link
Brakes front/rear	Discs/discs
Length	4821 mm (189.8 in.)
Width	1821 mm (71.7 in.)
Height	1425 mm (56.1 in.)
Wheelbase	2850 mm (112.2 in.)

The GS is the beginning of a new sculptural styling direction for Lexus. The front end adopts a cheerful expression with headlamps that wrap around the edges rearward like those on a Saab. These are low in relation to the rear of the car; a line from the back of the headlamps rises quickly to the A-pillar and waist to set up the side-window line. The cabin is set back behind the long bonnet and a slingshot quarter-window has been placed behind the division bar on the rear door, echoing classic sports-saloon proportions – Jaguar, mostly. The well-defined shoulder that runs the length of the waist gives the car a solid appearance and, coupled with handsome 18 in. wheels, a sense of progression.

The new interior is supposed, says Lexus, to offer comfort and relaxation. But the choice of a dark-grey dashboard and dark wood is not exactly soothing, and the sculpted surfaces could be softer to be much easier on the eye. The interior is actually quite sporty, with the three prominent, Alfa Romeo-style tunnelled instruments directly behind the steering wheel.

The GS comes with some of the latest technology. Keyless access means the driver can lock and unlock the car by touching the door handle and then press a push-button to start it; adaptive headlamps help illuminate a turn or curve as the driver steers into it; and a pre-collision system uses radar to detect obstacles in front of the car and determines whether a collision is unavoidable – it then retracts the front seatbelts and prepares the brake assist system.

Lexus LF-S and LF-X

Two new Lexus concept cars were launched at the Tokyo Motor Show in 2003, to pave the way for the long-awaited launch of the Lexus brand in Japan in August 2005. It's true: since its debut in 1989 Toyota's Lexus has been for alien consumption only, the Lexus GS300 and LS400 being sold in Japan as the Toyota Aristo and Celsior respectively.

The LF-S (shown opposite) is the saloon and the LF-X (shown above) is a closely related SUV sports-saloon crossover. The specification table given is for the LF-S, with the LF-X differing only slightly in being 25 mm (1 in.) longer, 90 mm (3.5 in.) wider and 300 mm (12 in.) higher. Both concepts aim to present a luxury view of Lexus and do so quite convincingly, with the bold grille up front and sweeping headlamps that contain the twin piercing, circular reflectors within.

The front view is unique, with a large shoulder formed by the headlamp profile that runs rearward along the waistline. Although the bonnet rises sharply up to the base of the windscreen, the drop-off on to the wing is large and so would result in limited-suspension travel and, hence, a sporty ride, particularly in the LF-S saloon.

Along the bodyside there is still work to do to complete practical detailing such as door rubbing strips and functional door handles. Also, the rear-door glass is bigger than the space in the door, so would not drop – a division bar would therefore be needed. The rear pillar slopes steeply and wraps around on to the rear screen like a coupé's, accentuating the sportiness of the saloon, while the rear lamps are small and have a neat wedge shape to them that signifies movement even when the car is standing still.

There is no reason why these models should have only Japanese appeal, so let's hope they have a global roll-out some time very soon.

Engine	4.3 V8 with hybrid electric power
Installation	Front-engined/four-wheel drive
Length	4910 mm (193.3 in.)
Width	1895 mm (74.6 in.)
Height	1345 mm (53 in.)

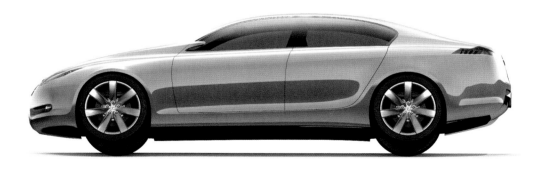

Lincoln Aviator

Design	David Woodhouse
Engine	3.5 V6
Power	183 kW (245 bhp)
Torque	326 Nm (240 lb. ft.)
Gearbox	6-speed automatic
Installation	Front-engined/all-wheel drive
Front suspension	MacPherson strut
Rear suspension	Multi-link
Brakes front/rear	Discs/discs
Front tyres	R21
Rear tyres	R21

The Aviator concept from Lincoln would be the Ford division's first car-based (instead of truck-based) SUV, tilted towards the mid-sized SUV segment, one of the fastest-growing in the industry, where the global sales pace is probably set by the Toyota Land Cruiser.

The signature bright metal strip that begins at the grille runs over the wings and then frames the full-length glass roof before ending at the lower tailgate. This is inspired by the 1961 Lincoln Continental and accentuates the car's profile. The egg-crate grille extends outboard, surrounding the headlamps, in another '61 Continental cue.

The all-glass roof provides a panoramic overhead view. At the rear of the roof, the wide C-pillar drops down, giving a sense of presence. At the rear, the glass bends horizontally at the waistline down on to horizontal tail lamps that stretch the full breadth of the rear, and emphasize the width. The exterior colour of the car appears to be black but, up close, its tone changes to a deep Pacific blue.

With a name like Aviator, you would probably expect aircraft-inspired fittings. It's all here. Four reclining, captain-style chairs have integral legrests for extra comfort and luxury. To complete the travel experience, DVD screens are integrated into the front seatbacks. A lighter-coloured leather is used above the interior waistline, helping to lift attention upward. The reddish undertones of the dark leather used from this point downward give the interior space a feeling of richness, while a hardwood floor with bright aluminium accents begins at the instrument panel and flows into the cargo space, visually maximizing the interior space out through to the inner tailgate.

Lincoln Mark X

Design	Marek Reichman
Engine	3.9 V8
Gearbox	5-speed automatic
Installation	Front-engined/rear-wheel drive
Brakes front/rear	Discs/discs
Front tyres	245/40R19
Rear tyres	275/35R19
Length	4701 mm (185 in.)
Width	1838 mm (72.4 in.)
Height	1302 mm (51.3 in.)
Wheelbase	2764 mm (108.8 in.)
Track front/rear	1552/1548 mm (61.1/60.9 in.)
Top speed	233 km/h (145 mph)

Throughout much of its history, Lincoln has used the 'Mark' nomenclature, beginning with the 1956 Continental Mark II that followed on from Edsel Ford's first Continental of 1939. Mark X, pronounced 'Mark 10', is Lincoln's first convertible with a power-folding, retractable glass hard-top. Following on from other recent Lincoln concepts, the Mark X uses rich materials with varying textures and contrasting colours to hammer home the brand's new design philosophy.

The exterior is uncluttered and has a feeling of powerful serenity to it. The detailing is subtle apart from the dominating grille, which, along with the headlights, looks as though it was lifted from one of Lincoln's dreadful 1970s leviathans, and occupies a good half of the frontal view. Still, coupled with the long bonnet, this chrome throwback suggests a powerful car that can waft the occupants along in enormous comfort. Delicate touches impress, such as the chrome trim that runs the length of the waistline, the inset door handles and the thin door mirrors.

Inside, a contrasting lime-green colour and textured materials present a modern and luxurious cabin, which uses white Corian accents, polished aluminium, dark chrome, natural-grain leather seating, plush sheepskin flooring and tailored stitching throughout.

The concept of a luxurious convertible lends itself perfectly to the new Lincoln design DNA, and it can be easily imagined sweeping along the American highways of our imagination. Nevertheless, with so modern an aura, the inclusion of such forgettable past design references at the front seems clumsy.

Maserati Quattroporte

Design	Pininfarina
Engine	4.2 V8
Power	298 kW (400 bhp) @ 7000 rpm
Torque	451 Nm (332 lb. ft.) @ 4500 rpm
Gearbox	6-speed clutchless manual
Installation	Front-engined/rear-wheel drive
Front suspension	Double wishbone
Rear suspension	Double wishbone
Brakes front/rear	Discs/discs
Front tyres	245/45ZR18
Rear tyres	285/45ZR18
Length	5052 mm (198.9 in.)
Width	1895 mm (74.6 in.)
Height	1438 mm (56.6 in.)
Wheelbase	3064 mm (120.6 in.)
Track front/rear	1587/1560 mm (62.5/61.4 in.)
Kerb weight	1860 kg (4100 lb.)
0–100 km/h (62 mph)	5.2 sec
Top speed	275 km/h (171 mph)

The new Quattroporte is the first production Maserati that Pininfarina has designed in fifty years. The great Battista 'Pinin' Farina himself (the founder's nickname and surname were united in 1961 by Italian government decree as both a company name and a surname for the coachbuilding dynasty) helped create some extraordinary one-off sports cars for the marque in the late 1940s and early 1950s, the last of which was a series of four A6GCS Berlinetta Sports in 1953. After that, Pininfarina worked prominently for Ferrari, Maserati's greatest competitor of the time, and Maserati turned to a less ritzy – and, no doubt, cheaper – stylist called Pietro Frua. He created the first Maserati Quattroporte (meaning 'four-door') in 1963, then considered a daring move.

This new Quattroporte's styling is unmistakably Italian. It's both elegant and powerful, while its soft overall forms are broken here and there by crease lines that create a real sense of tension. The Quattroporte was designed over an uncommonly long wheelbase with a cab-back stance that highlights the length of the bonnet and so emphasizes power. The imposing details of the grille and the C-pillar, the latter affording a certain amount of privacy to the occupants as befits a limousine, are all part and parcel of the Maserati tradition.

The side profile is dynamic, thanks to the short front overhang achieved by a transaxle layout, and the low front wing line, while the rear wheels are set in a muscular volume beneath that characterfully triangular C-pillar. The three small rectangular air vents in the front wings pay homage to Pininfarina's 1947 A6/1500 Berlinetta Speciale, while at the back the two rear-light clusters clearly echo the oval shape of the classic Maserati trident logo.

The cabin is beautifully fitted out in de luxe woods and leathers. All four seats are electrically adjustable and there's both a refrigeration compartment nestling in the front armrest and an electric sunshade for the rear window.

This new Maserati is the really design-concious choice for anyone who might normally buy the usual range of predictable German or British super-executive saloons. As such, it gets a warm welcome.

Mazda 3

Design	Moray Callum
Engine	2.0 in-line 4 (1.6 also offered)
Power	110 kW (147.5 bhp) @ 6000 rpm
Torque	187 Nm (137.8 lb. ft.) @ 4500 rpm
Gearbox	5-speed manual
Installation	Front-engined/front-wheel drive
Front suspension	MacPherson strut
Rear suspension	Multi-link
Brakes front/rear	Discs/discs
Front tyres	205/55R16
Rear tyres	205/55R16
Length	4420 mm (174 in.)
Width	1755 mm (69.1 in.)
Height	1465 mm (57.7 in.)
Wheelbase	2640 mm (103.9 in.)
Track front/rear	1530/1515 mm (60.2/59.6 in.)
Kerb weight	1310 kg (2888 lb.)
0–100 km/h (62 mph)	9 sec
Top speed	200 km/h (124 mph)
Fuel consumption	8.2 l/100 km (34.5 mpg)
CO_2 emissions	196 g/km

The new Mazda3 is available as either a five-door hatchback or a four-door saloon. The exterior looks rather dynamic, especially at the front, with its pointed, 'smiling' grille and lower air intake together with the sharp feature lines that form shoulders across the bonnet. Everything appears to triangulate off from the tip of the grille, including the headlamps complete with their piercing lenses, and there's quite a lot of plan curvature at the front end.

Mazda would, of course, be delighted to see its global advertising slogan mentioned, but there *is* definitely some 'zoom-zoom' motion, Mazda's new-found design DNA, to this car. Still, divide the car up into three equal sections front-to-rear and the rearmost portion, with its sloping roof, is just not as confident as the rest of the car, with its solid, sporty character.

This rear third of the Mazda3 is dominated by triangular C-pillars and fixed glass. The flared wings cut through along the doors, drawing the eye to the slightly bulging wheel arches that say 'power'. Taut surfaces with V-shaped design lines appear to emanate from the centrally positioned Mazda badge. The combination tail lamps are messy but this is today's vogue in lamp design.

Inside, the driving environment is overtly sporty, with prominent dials and a small leather gearstick, and there's a definite aura of quality about the switchgear.

Mazda Ibuki

Design	Moray Callum
Engine	1.6 in-line 4
Power	132 kW (177 bhp) @ 7500 rpm
Torque	180 Nm (133 lb. ft.) @ 6000 rpm
Gearbox	6-speed manual
Installation	Front-engined/front-wheel drive
Front suspension	Double wishbone
Rear suspension	Multi-link
Brakes front/rear	Discs/discs
Front tyres	215/40R18
Rear tyres	215/40R18
Length	3640 mm (143.3 in.)
Width	1720 mm (67.7 in.)
Height	1230 mm (48.4 in.)
Wheelbase	2330 mm (91.7 in.)
Track front/rear	1490/1495 mm (58.7/58.9 in.)

The Ibuki concept is a design study for a possible new lightweight roadster from Mazda that could become the new MX-5. The word *ibuki* means 'breathing new energy into, adding vigour' in Japanese. The overall design combines the original MX-5 with a futuristic vision for a Mazda open-top sports car.

The overall form has a distinct lozenge shape to it both from the side and from above. These lozenge shapes are then used to define individual features such as the headlamps and rear lamps, the bonnet recess and the front air intake in the bumper.

The huge 18 in. wheels positioned right at the corners help to evoke a real sense of driving fun, which is also illustrated by the highly technical interior that takes a rearward-biased position in the car.

There is a backbone chassis structure to the Ibuki that is reflected in the design of both the interior and the exterior. A smooth transition is visible between the exterior and interior, created by the brushed-aluminium strip that runs the length of the interior and extends beyond it into the bonnet recess and rear-ward into the roof stowage cover.

New hi-tech features include LED headlamps and keyless entry by ID card, while other innovations include a side-parting boot offering wide access. An advance in the audio system combines the seat air-conditioner ducts and speakers in one.

This is an exciting development from Mazda, generating great anticipation about what further concepts or production versions might follow.

Mazda Kusabi

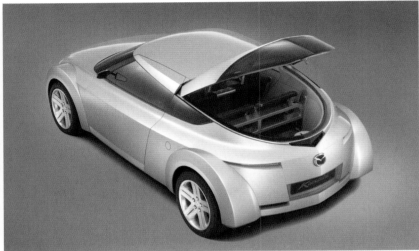

Design	Moray Callum
Engine	1.6 in-line 4 diesel
Power	80 kW (107 bhp) @ 4000 rpm
Torque	240 Nm (177 lb. ft.) @ 1750 rpm
Gearbox	6-speed automatic
Installation	Front-engined/front-wheel drive
Front suspension	MacPherson strut
Rear suspension	Torsion beam
Brakes front/rear	Discs/discs
Front tyres	205/50R17
Rear tyres	205/50R17
Length	3800 mm (149.6 in.)
Width	1750 mm (68.9 in.)
Height	1290 mm (50.8 in.)
Wheelbase	2490 mm (98 in.)
Track front/rear	1545/1545 mm (60.8/60.8 in.)

This sporty sub-compact car is derived from the Mazda2 platform. In Japanese, *kusabi* means 'wedge', a perfect name for the car's shape perhaps, but is it a perfect design for a car? It's certainly a profile that saw its apogee in the 1970s days of such stylistic horrors as the Triumph TR7.

The sloping roof gives the Kusabi its wedge shape, and, combined with the side and rear windows, an X-shaped C-pillar complete with two more wedges is created.

The exterior proportions are of a compact car with short overhangs, a forward-positioned windscreen and a dramatic sloping roofline. Because of this roofline, Mazda has cut the doors into the roof to allow the necessary clearance for occupants. At the rear is a twin-lift hatchback arrangement that opens individually on a hinge mounted longitudinally in the centre of the roof. The car looks chiselled and youthful, certainly, but it lacks sophistication and design refinement – certainly in terms of showroom cars.

The bold if rather simplistic front end has a wider, more intricate update of Mazda's signature five-point grille, while the headlamps have high-luminance LEDs located within small slotted openings. The huge, prominent wheel arches draw the eye to the 17 in. wheels although, with a 1.6 litre diesel engine, the Kusabi isn't going to be going particularly fast. The interior features an architectural instrument panel mounted within an aluminium frame that forms a ring frame around the footwell.

The Kusabi is a car to stimulate the senses and, although it's quite unlike any other Mazda, or concept car for that matter, it's hard to see how this can be anything other than a run-of-the-mill design exercise.

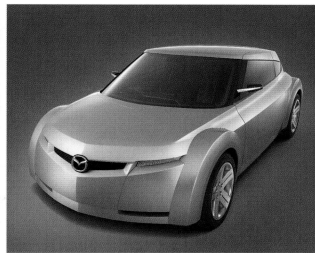

Mazda MX-Flexa

Design	Moray Callum
Engine	2.3 in-line 4
Power	126 kW (168 bhp) @ 6500 rpm
Torque	214 Nm (158 lb. ft.) @ 4000 rpm
Gearbox	Four-speed automatic
Installation	Front-engined/front-wheel drive
Front suspension	MacPherson strut
Rear suspension	Multi-link
Brakes front/rear	Discs/discs
Front tyres	235/50R18
Rear tyres	235/50R18
Length	4470 mm (176 in.)
Width	1745 mm (68.7 in.)
Height	1650 mm (65 in.)
Wheelbase	2750 mm (108.3 in.)
Track front/rear	1540/1525 mm (60.6/60 in.)

The Mazda MX-Flexa is an uncluttered and aerodynamic people-carrier directly derived from the Mazda3 platform. The A-pillars are positioned well forward, to maximize the six-seater's interior space. The body architecture is structured using two simple elements, a lower wedge and an upper curve, both joined by glazing from front to back. There is not much evident decoration. Indeed, the body does without the usual rubbing strips (no doubt this would be to the annoyance of customers in real life), with the height of the doors split only by a lower trim that skirts around the bottom of the whole car in a slightly darker shade of blue than the main coachwork.

At the front, the distinctive, angular and rising grille and swept-back headlamps mould into the body, a vertical line breaking them and providing the bumper-to-wing joint. This rises to create a bonnet shoulder then runs rearward to create the daylight opening line.

Inside, the dashboard is made up of vertical bands in contrasting colours of dark and light grey. The spirited Mazda ethos is emphasized by the slick, aluminium centre console and the luminous turquoise gauges that sit on the centre stack. The main instruments behind the steering wheel, both of which have a darker band running around the perimeter, echo the two-tone bodywork.

With sliding rear doors for practicality and bulletproof Japanese reliability, the MX-Flexa will be a hit in this growing sector when it goes into production very soon, probably as the Mazda4, and is likely to be barely altered from the car you see here.

Mazda MX-Micro Sport

Engine	2.0 in-line 4
Power	110 kW (148 bhp) @ 6500 rpm
Torque	183 Nm (135 lb. ft.) @ 4500 rpm
Gearbox	6-speed manual
Front suspension	MacPherson strut
Rear suspension	Torsion beam
Brakes front/rear	Discs/discs
Front tyres	205/50R17
Rear tyres	205/50R17
Length	3980 mm (156.7 in.)
Width	1755 mm (69 in.)
Height	1550 mm (61 in.)
Wheelbase	2490 mm (98 in.)
Track front/rear	1530/1550 mm (60.2/61 in.)

The exterior of the MX-Micro Sport communicates an interesting tension between the spacious, boxy cabin and the smaller, more curvaceous engine compartment. The headlamps are extremely dominating and lead the eye outward on to a strong, well-defined shoulder line that runs the length of the car. Also along the side are the large wheel arches that frame the wheels and suggest sportiness. The large air intake in the front bumper and bold vertical slits add to this mildly aggressive look.

The rear features combination lamps that echo the headlamp design. Sitting low down at the back are a racing-inspired airflow diffuser, vertical slits at either end of the bumper, and centrally located dual exhaust pipes, all to emphasize to motorists behind its added sporting persona.

Inside the MX-Micro, the interior mixes black and brown leather, highlighted with a red pinstripe that adds a touch of sophistication to what is otherwise a rather dark, Germanic cabin. The instrument panel's central section incorporates a reflective silver finish that complements the large, black-on-white instruments. A prominent multi-function display sits to the right of the steering wheel, and is visible and easy to operate by both driver and passenger.

For those who like the eye-catching and slightly quirky MX-Micro, there's good news indeed: a production version will make its debut late in 2004.

Mercedes-Benz CLS Coupé

Design	Peter Pfeiffer
Engine	5.0 V8 (3.5 V6 also offered)
Power	228 kW (306 bhp) @ 5600 rpm
Torque	460 Nm (339 lb. ft.) @ 2700-4250 rpm
Gearbox	7-speed automatic
Installation	Front-engined/all-wheel drive
Front suspension	Four-link
Rear suspension	Multi-link
Brakes front/rear	Discs/discs
Front tyres	255/40R18
Rear tyres	255/40R18
Length	4913 mm (193.4 in.)
Width	1851 mm (72.9 in.)
Height	1381 mm (54.4 in.)
Wheelbase	2854 mm (112.4 in.)
Track front/rear	1593/1603 mm (62.7/63 in.)
Kerb weight	1810 kg (3990 lb.)
0-100 km/h (62 mph)	6.1 sec
Top speed	250 km/h (155 mph) limited
Fuel consumption	11.3 l/100 km (25 mpg)

This four-door coupé is a new idea from Mercedes, a hybrid of luxury saloon and sports coupé. Once again, though, it's actually a format that made its debut decades ago: Britain's Rover was the pioneer of the four-door coupé with its low-roof version of the iconic P5 in 1962.

The CLS Coupé offers impressive proportions that are dictated by large overhangs, a smooth and sweeping silhouette with a taut coupé-style roof, frameless doors and an alluringly low-slung appearance. The headlamps and the radiator grille, with its distinctive vanes and centrally positioned star motif, remain prominent features, defining the classic Mercedes face. There is a feeling of thrust even when the car is stationary, created by the long sloping front and tyre-hugging wheel arches – Mercedes design typically combines taut lines and smooth rounded forms. The CLS has a distinct waistline that accentuates the height of the body at window level and gives an unmistakable appearance of strength.

As with all Mercedes models of this size, you would expect it to be loaded with features complete with a suitcase of nifty new tags. And they're all here: Active Light System, Cornering Light, Sensotronic Brake Control and the world's first seven-speed automatic transmission for a production passenger car. There are also Softstop, for stopping smoothly in heavy traffic, Anti-Stall Assist, to make hill starts easier, and Tailback Assist, an aid that enables drivers to apply the brakes in stop-and-go traffic simply by releasing the accelerator.

The interior is impressive too; leather and wood are the main interior-design elements, with only subtle tonal differences between them. The diamond-shaped grain of the beige-coloured leather on the seats is a neat touch.

Mercedes-Benz's hype machine at Frankfurt led to the belief that the concept model had a high possibility of being unleashed for public consumption. Now we have confirmation, after an apparently rapturous reception from potential buyers, that the 'CLS Class' is a reality. It gives the marque yet another luxury choice to add to its line-up, and something to irk rivals such as BMW or Lexus, or even Rover.

Mercedes-Benz F500 Mind

The new F500 Mind research vehicle demonstrates several new technologies showcased in advance of being made available on regular Mercedes-Benz production cars.

The design is heavily wedge-shaped with a rearward-biased body mass. The door waistlines rise sharply up over the roof to form a reinforced roof bar. Because of the extraordinary rear-door profile and Mercedes' desire for a fully glazed upper structure, there are no less than five separate glazed panels on each side.

The rear door can be opened either conventionally or on rear hinges. There is a lower B-pillar that swings as part of the door when rear-hinged, and that acts as a B-pillar structure when conventionally front-hinged. In reality this would be extremely difficult to make work effectively, being far too complex a system.

Inside the cockpit is a multi-vision display. The dials and gauges in the instrument cluster are programmable, their images projected through a semi-transparent mirror to highlight the most relevant information of the moment. A voice-operated control system is installed that uses ultrasonic technology: this directs sounds from the navigation system at the driver only, so the front and rear passengers remain undisturbed.

At night or in low light, a night-vision system projects images on to the multi-vision display. This consists of two infrared laser headlamps on the front of the vehicle and a windscreen-mounted camera that illuminate and scan the road ahead for a distance of up to 150 m (490 ft.).

If anyone can successfully implement this technology in production then Mercedes-Benz can, but this is one car you'll certainly never be able to fix in your garage at the weekend.

Power	234 kW (314 bhp)
Length	5092 mm (200 in.)
Wheelbase	2965 mm (116.7 in.)

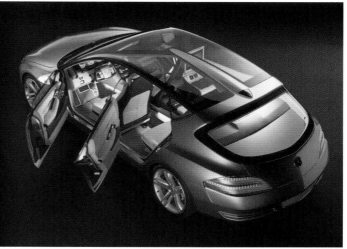

Mercedes-Benz SLK

Engine	5.5 V8 (1.8 in-line 4 and 3.5 V6 also offered)
Power	268 kW (360 bhp) @ 5750 rpm
Torque	510 Nm (376 lb. ft.) @ 4000 rpm
Gearbox	7-speed automatic
Installation	Front-engined/rear-wheel drive
Front suspension	MacPherson strut
Rear suspension	Multi-link
Brakes front/rear	Discs/discs
Front tyres	225/40R18
Rear tyres	245/35R18
Length	4087 mm (160.9 in.)
Width	1794 mm (70.6 in.)
Height	1271 mm (50 in.)
Wheelbase	2430 mm (95.7 in.)
Track front/rear	1524/1549 mm (60/61 in.)
Kerb weight	1540 kg (3395 lb.)
0–100 km/h (62 mph)	4.9 sec
Top speed	250 km/h (155 mph) limited
Fuel consumption	12 l/100 km (25.5 mpg)

The new SLK Class takes design inspiration from the new SLR supercar and is much more evocative than the outgoing model, which always appeared a bit truncated at the front with its rectangular headlamps. Nevertheless, the original SLK, introduced in 1996 and, at the time, the shortest car Mecedes-Benz had ever produced, was a real hit with monied buyers.

The new model is a more masculine and powerful-looking car than the preceding model. It sports large wheels, muscular shoulders and a dynamic wedge shape. The long bonnet complete with the raised centre section gives the SLK a fresh yet still familiar face. The grille has two chrome wings that split the dark opening and lead the eye outboard to the leant-back headlamps that cut across the bonnet and wings.

From the side, the SLK's long bonnet, raked A-pillars, wide doors and short rear end are typical road-ster features. The body is 72 mm (2.8 in.) wider than the old SLK's and this is used to add wheel arch flair and to emphasize a sporty nature. A rising feature line beginning at the front of the door arches upward and rearward, gradually gaining definition until it reaches the edge of the tail lamp.

Inside, the dashboard looks sporty and exudes technicality. The silver-coloured controls are visually lifted from the black surfaces on the steering wheel, centre console and transmission tunnel. The two large, elliptical instruments behind the steering wheel have silver-painted tubes surrounding each of them.

The car-design community feels that Mercedes-Benz has been able to get the masculine/feminine balance right on the level for the new SLK, so it should now appeal equally to both sexes, rather than being slightly derided by some men as too 'soft'.

Mercedes-Benz SLR McLaren

Design	Gordon Murray
Engine	5.4 V8
Power	460 kW (617 bhp) @ 6500 rpm
Torque	780 Nm (575 lb. ft.) @ 3250–5000 rpm
Gearbox	5-speed automatic
Installation	Front-engined/all-wheel drive
Front suspension	Double wishbone
Rear suspension	Double wishbone
Brakes front/rear	Discs/discs
Front tyres	245/40R18
Rear tyres	245/40R18
Length	4656 mm (183.3 in.)
Width	1908 mm (75.1 in.)
Height	1261 mm (49.6 in.)
Wheelbase	2700 mm (106.3 in.)
Track front/rear	1638/1569 mm (64.5/61.8 in.)
Kerb weight	1768 kg (3898 lb.)
0–100 km/h (62 mph)	3.8 sec
Top speed	334 km/h (208 mph)
Fuel consumption	14.8 l/100 km (19.1 mpg)

Finally, the new Mercedes-Benz SLR McLaren has been launched in its customer-ready form. This project has been extremely challenging, even with the combined skills of a Mercedes-Benz/McLaren team.

The two-seater SLR has striking 'swing-wing' doors and styling elements borrowed from the historic Formula 1 Silver Arrows racers; it builds on the legacy of the famous SLR race cars of the 1950s. The proportion is of a cab-rearward design, very necessary owing to the size of the powertrain. Similarly, the Mercedes twin-headlamp nose comes with huge air intakes for cooling its beast of an engine. The body sits like a low, thin wedge and features many arrow-shaped details so that you're left in no doubt that this is a very fast car indeed. The elaborate slats behind the front wheels and the pointed front edge to the rear lamp both suggest extreme forward motion.

The blend of technologies is a heady cocktail of rock-solid Mercedes road cars and fire-breathing McLaren F1 racing machines: both safety and performance are intrinsic to the design. The body is made from carbon fibre composite; this lightweight material has excellent energy absorption properties in a crash and incredibly high specific stiffness and strength. The result is a car with high stiffness and low weight. A little-known challenge has been to achieve a top-class paint finish on carbon fibre.

Aerodynamics plays a central part in supercar design, and the SLR has a virtually smooth underbody with a six-channel diffuser at the rear just like in F1. An additional adaptive spoiler gives extra downforce: from 95 km/h (59 mph) it adopts a 10-degree raised position, increasing pressure over the rear axle. It also doubles as an airbrake when the driver brakes heavily, rising instantly to an angle of 65 degrees.

Details are everything inside. Perhaps the most entertaining one is the starter button on the metal shift knob at the top of the gearshift lever, which immediately glows red when the key is inserted.

This is not a profitable project for Mercedes-Benz, which is bankrolling it. Revenue will never even remotely equal development costs – a financial scenario with which McLaren, at least, is all too familiar from the days of the F1 road-car project, a famous loss-maker. But for the privileged future owners, this is an amazing technological marvel to have outside the French château or Malibu beachfront retreat.

Mercedes-Benz Vision GST

Engine	3.2 in-line 6
Power	234 kW (314 bhp)
Torque	860 Nm (634 lb. ft.)
Installation	Front-engined/four-wheel drive
Front suspension	Double wishbone
Rear suspension	Four-link
Brakes front/rear	Discs/discs
Front tyres	255/30R21
Rear tyres	295/30R21
Length	5130 mm (202 in.)
Width	1922 mm (75.7 in.)
Height	1648 mm (64.5 in.)
Wheelbase	3215 mm (126.6 in.)
0–100 km/h (62 mph)	6.6 sec
Top speed	250 km/h (155 mph) limited
Fuel consumption	9.4 l/100 km (30 mpg)

This is the last concept iteration we shall see of the Mercedes GST before it goes into full production in 2005. The Vision Grand Sports Tourer has a number of interesting changes from the original concept shown two years earlier and featured in *The Car Design Yearbook 1*, mainly to ensure a more user-friendly and – importantly – production-feasible design. These include new, larger door handles, and a cant rail that now runs horizontally along the top of the rear door; this improves ingress but, unfortunately, breaks the harmonious appearance of the arc of the earlier concept. A division bar has been added in to the rear-door glass, allowing the side window to drop, and the sporty airscoop is now removed from the bottom of the rear door. It has to be said that the overall look is less dynamic than that of the original concept, and this is down to the altered side-window profile – a shame.

Taut, rising lines and a streamlined body give the GST an arrow-like profile. Three metallic horizontal slats sit around the Mercedes star symbol, and splay out to the oval headlamps, all of which gives the car visual width at the front. At the back, the striking tail lights and full-width rear screen make the GST appear wide with a spacious interior. The glass roof lets light flood in, creating a feeling of transparency.

It may have lost an element of pure aesthetic from the original concept, but the final GST design is as true to its siring concept as it was possible to be within practical limitations; such is life for cars in the real world.

Mitsubishi Colt

Engine	1.5 in-line 4 (1.1 and 1.3 in-line 3, and 1.5 in-line 3 diesel, also offered)
Power	81 kW (109 bhp)
Torque	145 Nm (107 lb. ft.)
Gearbox	5-speed manual
Installation	Front-engined/front-wheel drive
Front suspension	MacPherson strut
Rear suspension	Torsion beam
Brakes front/rear	Discs/discs
Front tyres	195/50R15
Rear tyres	195/50R15
Length	3870 mm (152.4 in.)
Width	1695 mm (66.7 in.)
Height	1550 mm (61 in.)
Wheelbase	2500 mm (98.4 in.)
Track front/rear	1450/1445 mm (57/56.9 in.)
Kerb weight	1090 kg (2403 lb.)

Based on the CZ3 concept car, launched in late 2001, the new Colt sits squarely in the European small hatchback B-segment and retains a tamely feminine appearance, with what is essentially a mono-volume. Taut surfaces and body-coloured trim maximize its perceived size.

The body style is really quite uninspiring, if wholly practical, and only the headlamps and tail lamps add any emotional spirit to what is otherwise a bland piece of car design. The three-diamond Mitsubishi logo sits on a triangular plinth that naturally sets up an angled grille and angular headlamps, a look that is now a trademark of Mitsubishi's design identity. Along the side, the multiple body-coloured upper pillars do nothing to create a feeling of openness in the cabin, although there was clearly a move towards this with both front and rear quarter-glass windows; instead, at least from the outside, they create a boxed-in appearance.

The interior is dark and sporty in two-tone colours with bright aluminium switches that stand out. The instrumentation, vents and switchgear have a circular theme that is clear and approachable in layout.

The new Colt might be a practical choice for some buyers but there are more exciting alternatives in competition with it.

Mitsubishi Eclipse Concept-E

Engine	3.8 V6 and electric motor
Power	355 kW (476 bhp)
Gearbox	6-speed automated manual
Installation	Front-engined/four-wheel drive
Front suspension	MacPherson strut
Rear suspension	Multi-link
Brakes front/rear	Discs/discs
Front tyres	245/40R20
Rear tyres	275/35R20
Length	4320 mm (170 in.)
Width	1855 mm (73 in.)
Height	1300 mm (51.2 in.)
Wheelbase	2635 mm (103.7 in.)
Track front/rear	1570/1560 mm (61.8/61.4 in.)

With a concept car output as prodigious as any Japanese manufacturer, Mitsubishi nonetheless struggles to make much impact with its work. So here's a pleasant surprise: the company has created a show car that's truly memorable – a compact, sporty coupé that sits somewhere between an Audi TT and a Porsche 911 Carrera, and could prove a worthy successor to the much-loved production FTO coupé. The taut, muscular exterior is let down only by a poorly finished interior.

With an overtly arched profile, the Eclipse Concept-E boasts cab-forward proportions and muscular surfaces that, from some angles, are pure Porsche. That cab-forward stance means the A-pillar is positioned on top of the front wheel arch and the side-window glass runs forward, creating a teardrop shape and a curved opening line at the front of the door. The gaping air intake in the front bumper shows how much air is needed to cool the trendy hybrid powertrain (V6 petrol engine and a 150 kW electric motor), and the triangular headlamps lead on to the bonnet to create a cross-brace effect that rises up to the windscreen. This trick has the effect of emphasizing the car's torsional stiffness and pin-sharp handling.

The glass roof runs over on to a semicircular rear screen. The airflow creates lift at the rear with this type of rear-end design treatment, so a spoiler is added that, visually, creates a bridge between the rear lamps. Inside, though, the teardrop profile is used throughout to negative effect: the colour choice is cold and unwelcoming and the use of unflattering textures does nothing to boost the car's desirability.

Designed at Mitsubishi's California studio, the Eclipse Concept-E brings Mitsubishi closer to the cutting edge, but a more rigorous approach – think German – is still needed for sports car perfection.

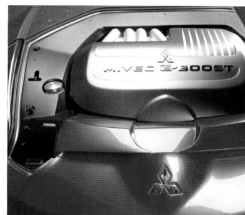

Mitsubishi Grandis

Design	Olivier Boulay
Engine	2.4 in-line 4
Power	123 kW (165 bhp) @ 6000 rpm
Torque	217 Nm (160 lb. ft.) @ 4000 rpm
Gearbox	5-speed manual
Installation	Front-engined/front-wheel drive
Front suspension	MacPherson strut
Rear suspension	Semi-trailing arm
Brakes front/rear	Discs/discs
Front tyres	215/60R16
Rear tyres	215/60R16
Length	4755 mm (187.2 in.)
Width	1795 mm (70.7 in.)
Height	1655 mm (65.2 in.)
Wheelbase	2830 mm (111.4 in.)
Track front/rear	1550/1555 mm (61/61.2 in.)
Kerb weight	1620 kg (3572 lb.)

Inspiration for the Grandis came from two previous Mitsubishi concept cars, the Space Liner and the CZ3 Tarmac. The Grandis blends the cool and comfortable from the Space Liner with the emotional and sporty from the Tarmac.

Back in the 1980s and early 1990s, the MPV was the in-thing. Since then, a whole raft of SUVs has taken the market centre stage, and the worthier MPV format has lost much of its novelty. Hence the Grandis aims to be lower and sportier and to appear sharper than its people-carrying competitors. It will be an additional model to the established Space Wagon MPV, but Mitsubishi says it will utilize a more dynamic design to position it very differently in the market. Oh, the confused machinations of the crossover car …

The headlamps are striking and echo the design of Mitsubishi's three-pointed star emblem. They set up the waistline, which finishes neatly at the rear lamps. The tapered roofline adds to the overall dynamism of its silhouette. The sculpted doors include a character line that runs upward at their base towards the rear bumper, to break up the slab-sidedness.

Inside, the dashboard and door panels have a wavy form. Peacefully pleasing to the eye, this boosts the feeling of roominess and the soothing sense of relaxation. The Grandis certainly stands out from the crowd: it looks thoroughly purposeful, a convincing new product.

Mitsubishi i

Design	Olivier Boulay
Engine	1.0 in-line 3
Power	50 kW (67 bhp) @ 6000 rpm
Torque	92 Nm (68 lb. ft.) @ 3500 rpm
Gearbox	CVT
Installation	Rear-engined/rear-wheel drive
Front suspension	MacPherson strut
Rear suspension	De Dion axle
Brakes front/rear	Discs/discs
Front tyres	145/65R15
Rear tyres	175/55R15
Length	3516 mm (138.4 in.)
Width	1505 mm (59.3 in.)
Height	1514 mm (59.6 in.)
Wheelbase	2560 mm (100.8 in.)
Track front/rear	1300/1280 mm (51.2/50.4 in.)
Kerb weight	790 kg (1742 lb.)
0–100 km/h (62 mph)	10.9 sec
Top speed	185 km/h (115 mph)
Fuel consumption	3.8 l/100 km (74 mpg)
CO$_2$ emissions	89 g/km

Could this really be Japan's answer to the MCC Smart City Coupé?

Well, not really: it's too large, for one thing. But it does share that elusive 'product design' feel – that use of playful design language, with almost no straight lines, that gives a static feel rather than the look of horizontal movement captured in most car design. It's more food processor than Ferrari, if you like. Similarities exist to the MCC Smart in its construction, too, with a featherlight aluminium body frame and various ultra-light plastics used for exterior cladding.

The name 'i' is, of course, symbolic, meaning 'myself' and 'love' (*ai* means love in Japanese), and also standing for 'innovation', 'imagination' and 'intelligence'. But then this is all Mitsubishi's self-loving marketing speak!

The control of natural light in the interior environment has been carefully considered. Generous amounts of it flood in through the roof and the large windows. The seats are made from a green transparent material, allowing light to penetrate to usually gloomy corners and, at the same time, creating a feeling of spaciousness. There's also a green light strip that glows in the middle of the dashboard at night, fitted with touchscreen control for audio and e-commerce functions.

For once, in concept car terms, Mitsubishi should be congratulated for being really bold: the i is scheduled to appear on the Japanese market in autumn 2005. Mitsubishi says it could later make its way to Europe as well. This model, with its appliance-like attributes, could do very well, but the surfaces would need to be tweaked just a bit to make it truly desirable for European tastes.

Mitsubishi Se-ro

It is an extraordinary concept – a combination of four-wheeled 'bubble car' straight out of the brave 1950s (who else remembers the Messerschmitt Tiger?) and something bang-up-to-date like a Smart. The Mitsubishi Se-ro defies current small-car conventions. The unpainted and polished aluminium body is too reflective to be practical for the road but it's another highly visual suggestion of an era when home-spun innovation contrasted with the space race and the aircraft's transition to the jet age. You feel nostalgic looking at the Se-ro, even if you don't quite know why!

The overall proportion is of a tall monospace with a blunt front end that curves radially in plan. There is a strong degree of symmetry, front to rear, particularly in the screens, the doors, the wheel arches and the overall profile. This makes for a playful look, again like a Smart, rather than the more prolific sporty one. The wheels are traditional 'hot rod' five-spokes with a simple engineered look that, unfortunately, does not sit well with the more 'organic' body-design language.

The detail features are richly expressive to make a strong product-design statement. With small changes such as making the 'dog leg' A-pillar smaller to improve visibility, Se-ro could be a production possibility and compete cheerfully in the morose city-car market. The engine and other powertrain components are positioned between the two axles to give a roomy interior, although that means the floor is raised higher than usual.

Mitsubishi's target market for the Se-ro is thirty-five-year-old males. It is proposed as a lifestyle concept for going to parties with friends or forming a private space for free-time activities such as getting away from the city and enjoying outdoor pursuits. The Se-ro seems too limited in space to achieve this in comfort, though.

The design will be awkward on the eye for many; some symmetries, such as the door glass, do not work, and lines flow into one another very abruptly. Yet this is all part of the fun of an organic design if it's going to stand out from the generally acceptable (for which read 'bland') crowd.

Engine	0.66 in-line 3
Gearbox	CVT
Installation	Mid-engined/rear-wheel drive
Length	3395 mm (133.7 in.)
Width	1475 mm (58 in.)
Height	1675 mm (65.9 in.)
Wheelbase	2560 mm (100.8 in.)

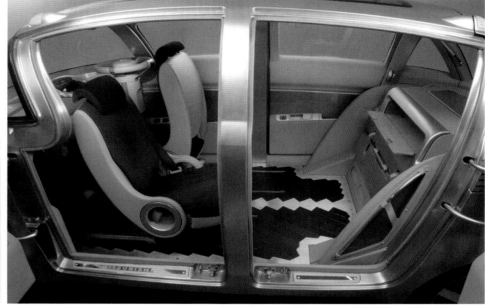

Mitsubishi Sport Truck

Engine	4.7 V8
Power	172 kW (231 bhp)
Gearbox	5-speed automatic
Installation	Front-engined/four-wheel drive
Front suspension	Double wishbone
Rear suspension	Multi-link
Brakes front/rear	Discs/discs
Front tyres	305/45R22
Rear tyres	305/45R22
Length	5255 mm (206.9 in.)
Width	1995 mm (78.5 in.)
Height	1770 mm (69.7 in.)
Wheelbase	3380 mm (133 in.)
Track front/rear	1640/1640 mm (64.6/64.6 in.)
Kerb weight	2000 kg (4409 lb.)

Emanating from California, the Sport Truck has a powerful and muscular design with a body that wraps the engine and huge wheels. Unlike some other trucks, however, such as the Honda SUT concept with its geometric design language, the Mitsubishi's body gives the appearance of a monocoque that moulds the cabin and load-bay area together in a sculpted way. Sadly, not only is the bodywork as a whole clumsy and unsophisticated-looking, but so are the gross wheel arches.

At the front, horizontal silver bands break up the height of the vehicle, and also make it look strong and tough. These bands are used throughout the exterior, especially around the side windows, drawing the bystander's gaze upward, and also feature inside the cabin. The headlamps sit above one of the silver bands, while the driving lamps sit below it, their shapes not exactly complementing each other, and making the front-end design even harder on the eye.

Inside are strong, linear forms that are more geometric than the exterior. The design language does not flow cleanly between exterior and interior, although there are metallic surfaces that highlight the sense of strength. The instrument cluster features an LCD display, the gear-selector is a simple dial, and paddle-type controls are located on the steering wheel.

Mitsubishi has designed much better concepts. This one at best doesn't even merit a place in its museum of past concepts – awful.

Nissan Actic

The Nissan Actic was created at Nissan's design studios in California. The spacy-looking hatchback uses gently flowing surfaces that adorn a streamlined shape, and also the clever matching trailer, broken only at the front by the pepper-pot grille.

Actic's proportions are characterized by a long wheelbase and short overhangs, the silhouette very similar to the influential Mercedes GST. There is no B-pillar: the front side doors slide forward and the rear ones backward to provide ample easy access. 'Smart' door handles sense the pass of a hand and present themselves for operation. Overhead, a glass-panelled roof uses in-built display screens to allow passengers to play video displays to the outside world (although why they would want to do that isn't made clear).

A tiny but important technological feature is at the heart of the car's concept. It's a keyfob that is actually a portable transmitting hard drive; it holds the passenger preferences, settings and configurations for not only the audio and HVAC (heating, ventilation and air-conditioning) but also e-mail and navigation settings. Again, weren't cars once intended for driving?

Following behind, the trailer includes an inflatable wall system that turns it into a space for sleeping three people. To show that the trailer has been designed specifically for the Actic, a built-in trailer-coupling arm is integrated into the rear styling of the Actic, allowing the car and trailer visibly to become one unit.

The Actic is one of those exciting concepts that transport you into the future, demonstrating new and exciting technologies within a style that could be only a few years away. Well, probably …

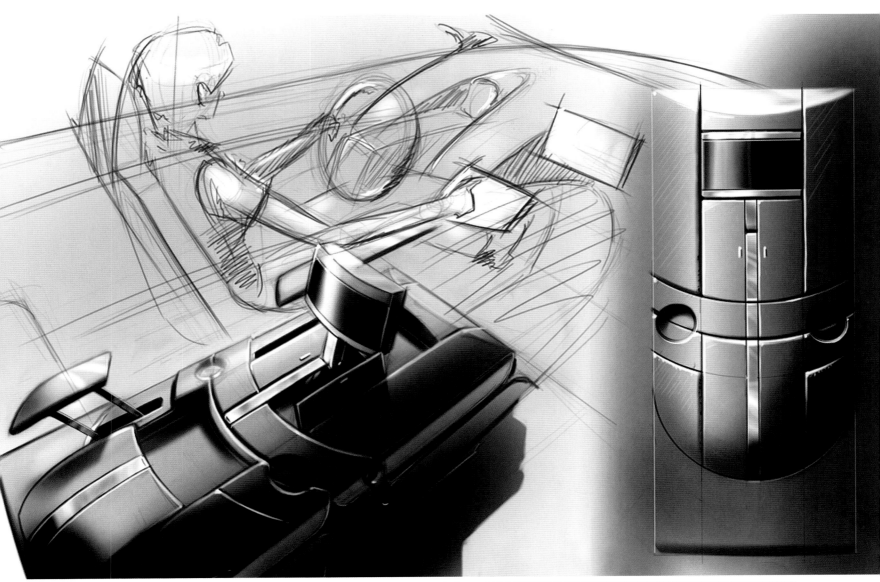

Nissan Conran Cube

Design	Conran & Partners
Installation	Front-engined / front-wheel drive
Front suspension	MacPherson strut
Rear suspension	Torsion beam
Front tyres	175 / 60R15
Rear tyres	175 / 60R15
Length	3900 mm (153.5 in.)
Width	1680 mm (66.1 in.)
Height	1645 mm (64.8 in.)
Wheelbase	2600 mm (102.4 in.)
Track front/rear	1470 / 1455 mm (57.9/57.3 in.)

Nissan worked together with Conran & Partners, the London-based design consultants, to design the Cube. Terence Conran, most famously known for setting up the Habitat homewares chain and introducing modern interior design to the masses, has for the first time turned his corporate hand to reworking an entire car, the Nissan Cube introduced in 2002.

By using Conran designers, you get a fusion between Terence Conran's design ethos – that of creating self-consciously upmarket, sophisticated lifestyles – and Nissan's engineering thoroughness. Conran has chosen a key element of Japan's national psyche, the calming influence, to orchestrate the design language of his Cube, believing that the circle best represents Japanese beauty. So it is the circle, together with pure straight lines, that defines every visible facet of the Cube's demeanour. This has worked well, although it projects a fashionable, modern design for right now, rather than a more complex classic with longevity.

The overall proportion is of a two-box shape complete with an upright windscreen and sides. At the front, the pepper-pot grille houses the circular lighting and creates a playful 'face'. At the rear the door spans the whole width of the car, very like a fridge door. Bright-red lozenge headrests show through the rear screen, symbolizing huge stop lamps. The full wheel covers are, Conran posits, inspired by the radiating water ripples from Japanese rock gardens. Inside, the air vents, gearstick and speaker grilles are all circular too.

To have design experts crossing disciplines like this is an excellent way to explore new ideas. It's unlikely that a production model could be conceived like this but it adds to the design stimulation of two very different creative industries. And those with long memories will recall that Conran's design bureau has been called upon by the automotive industry before: Land Rover worked with Conran on the interior of the 1989 Discovery SUV … with not especially distinguished results. When the hyperbole has cleared, there's not a great deal about pragmatic car design that the car-design community itself can't figure out.

Nissan Dunehawk

Nissan launched the Dunehawk at Frankfurt in 2003 – a bold concept car that hints suggestively at the future direction for Nissan SUVs. The chiselled architecture and the grey colour Nissan has chosen for the concept make it look as though it was hewn straight from a block of granite. Even the lamps are frosty white in colour to emphasize the don't-care coolness of the car.

The overall appearance is of a tough model, with powerful features at the front, including the chunky radiator surrounds and front underguard as well as the large bumper. Dunehawk positively towers on its enormous wheels to give suitable ground clearance and an elevated driving position; massive, gaping wheel arches provide plenty of scope for their articulation when travelling off-road. The waistline is very high and the recessed side windows add to the military-tough image created by the pronounced pillars along the side.

The chassis is equipped with the second generation of Nissan's all-mode four-wheel-drive system, first seen on the X-Trail. Inside the Dunehawk the appearance is of a car that's highly functional rather than cossetingly comfortable. The Dunehawk looks like it was designed specifically with California's new governor Mr Schwarzenegger in mind, so we can be fairly sure that a customer-ready version would go down a storm in the crucial American SUV market. It also provides plenty to lambast for those who think SUVs like this add to the perceived (and, probably, actual) menace of today's roadscape.

Installation	Front-engined / four-wheel drive
Length	4795 mm (188.8 in.)
Width	1900 mm (74.8 in.)
Wheelbase	2820 mm (111 in.)

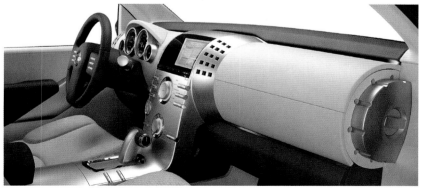

Nissan Effis

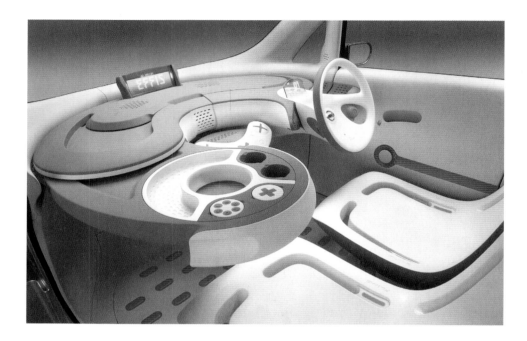

Engine	Electric motor
Installation	Four-wheel drive
Front tyres	165/55R15
Rear tyres	165/55R15
Length	3000 mm (118.1 in.)
Width	1600 mm (63 in.)
Height	1550 mm (61 in.)
Wheelbase	2050 mm (80.7 in.)

Here is a witty addition to Nissan's concept car range. The Effis is a fuel-cell car with the fuel-cell stack and battery under the floor to enhance interior roominess and help lower the centre of gravity. The hydrogen tank is located under the rear seat to achieve an overall length of 3 metres (10 ft.). Each motor features two drive-shafts that are controlled independently, so the driving force can be distributed separately to right and left wheels. As a result of this, says Nissan, there's no need for a conventional steering system.

When only the driver is on board, a rotary table can expand from the dashboard and be used as a de luxe cupholder or else function as, say, a map-reading surface. The driver can enter the car from either side, something made much easier because the steering wheel incorporates a tilting mechanism so that the effective space of the driver's seat can be increased.

One of the technical advances featured on the Effis demonstrates the lengths Nissan has gone to to save weight. The aluminium panels are unpainted, and instead are electrolytically coloured by giving them a chemical surface treatment combined with dyeing. This means the weight of a car's-worth of paint is saved. This sounds like a fantastic idea that could easily be put into production this afternoon, but the base panels would have to be of exceptional surface quality because painting normally covers up myriad tiny imperfections in panel quality.

Nissan has studied what makes for convenience in urban situations, and has designed the Effis concept with one driver-side door, two double-hinged doors on the passenger side, and only an openable glass hatch at the rear; luggage is accessed from either the glass hatch or the rear side door.

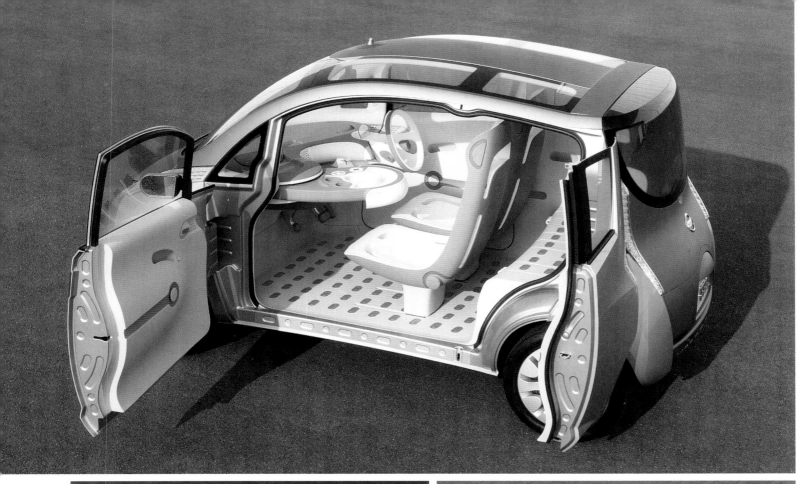

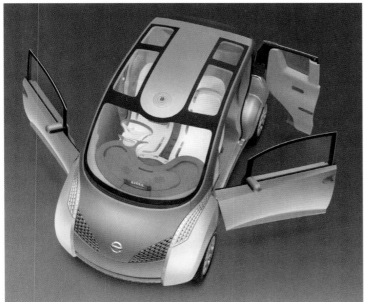

Nissan Frontier

Engine	4.0 V6 (2.5 in-line 4 also offered)
Power	186 kW (250 bhp)
Torque	366 Nm (270 lb. ft.)
Gearbox	5-speed automatic or 6-speed manual
Installation	Front-engined / four-wheel drive
Front suspension	Double wishbone
Rear suspension	Rigid leaf
Brakes front/rear	Discs / discs
Front tyres	265 / 65R17
Rear tyres	265 / 65R17
Length	5220 mm (205.5 in.)
Width	1849 mm (72.8 in.)
Height	1770 mm (69.7 in.)
Wheelbase	3198 mm (125.9 in.)

The Frontier sits in the 'compact truck' market segment in the United States and is offered with either a King Cab or a Crew Cab body style. Its bigger brother is the Titan, with which it shares the F-Alpha platform and other practical elements such as the suspension and the durable spray-in load-bed liner. By adopting this set-up, the Frontier benefits from the strength of a platform designed for a bigger truck, making it more durable and solid for its size.

The style of the Frontier is very utilitarian: large ground clearance, blistered geometric wheel arches with room for plenty of jerky suspension travel for off-roading, and skidplates front and rear to offer hull protection. Chrome bumpers, grille bars and door mirrors exude the feel of the manly US trucking environment that Nissan has successfully exploited. Climbing in and out of a Frontier is easy, helped by the upright windscreen and elevated body – a facet that American buyers revere, even if they rarely make use of the vehicle's true practicality and secretly curse the load-bed for offering none of the conventional security of a car boot. At the rear, the lamps are vertical and narrow, set right out at the edges to allow maximum width for the drop-down tailgate. The simple interior has been devised for hard workers, with large buttons that are easy to use when wearing gloves.

The Frontier is sure to be a big seller in the United States and will sit proudly alongside the full-sized Titan in a range gaining more and more Stateside credibility – Chevrolet, Dodge and Ford beware!

Nissan Fuga

Installation	Front-engined / rear-wheel drive
Brakes front/rear	Discs / discs
Front tyres	245 / 40R20
Rear tyres	245 / 40R20
Length	4930 mm (194 in.)
Width	1850 mm (72.8 in.)
Height	1510 mm (59.4 in.)
Wheelbase	2950 mm (116.1 in.)

A proposal for a top-line executive saloon that might compete against such models as the Volkswagen Phaeton: that's what the Nissan Fuga is supposed to be.

A classic three-box proportion defines the Fuga. Viewed from the side, there is a gently rising waistline along the car, while the roofline flows smoothly from roof to rear screen in a style reminiscent of a coupé. As a result, there's a short boot lid and a muscular-looking C-pillar. Aluminium detailing is used to give a sporty but still executive feel, and also draws the eye to key feature lines over the body that visually lengthen the car. It's low, elegant and smooth

The front grille is made up of six chrome strips, which signify intrinsic power bursting at the seams. The same graphic is echoed lower down in the front bumper. The headlamps and tail lamps both feature an L-shape form that makes an interesting surrounding to the twin internal rings.

The interior combines white cypress wood with white and black trim. This is then highlighted by aluminium dials that feature bright-blue backlighting. The effect is of sensory confusion between soft relaxation and harsh sportiness. The interior is bathed in soft indirect light coming through the twin roof lights, inspired by Japanese paper-covered slatted lamps.

With more care over the choice of interior colours and materials, the Fuga could sit easily and proudly within Nissan's (or, in the United States, Infiniti's) range.

Nissan Jikoo

Front tyres	195 / 50R20
Rear tyres	195 / 50R20
Length	3730 mm (146.9 in.)
Width	1615 mm (63.6 in.)
Height	1230 mm (48.4 in.)
Wheelbase	2400 mm (94.5 in.)

The launch of the Jikoo coincides not only with Nissan's seventieth anniversary but also with the four hundredth anniversary of the Edo Shogunate, involving a celebration of the achievements of traditional artisans from Tokyo (originally named Edo). The Jikoo is a small two-seater that is essentially a rolling design obsession with past and present, and which also pays homage to the original Datsun Roadster that made its debut in 1935, echoing its prominent bonnet, short cabin and overall silhouette.

Several traditional craft techniques are used on the Jikoo's components, making for an eclectic mix, including front wing trims made from hammered metal, which create the warm look of silver and complement the painted body. Headlamp design is based on the concept of light being transmitted through Japanese paper, while the rear lamps symbolize Edo cut glass.

The interior, combining gorgeous curves with geometric patterns, best evokes Edo crafts – it's a work of art. The black and vermilion tones of the interior trim come from expressive kabuki (traditional Japanese drama) costume. Although the fan-shaped dashboard is actually inspired by that pioneering Datsun, it is brought bang up to date with two large display screens positioned each side of the digital speedometer.

The passenger screen continually redisplays information about present-day and ancient Tokyo. City maps from the Edo period as well as information about historical events, culture and traditions all strive to bring local knowledge to the vehicle occupants. Such an information resource could perhaps be linked to a car's GPS system and then implemented into mainstream models.

Whether you consider the Jikoo to be a confused sports car or even a time machine, it has a number of human interfaces that will prompt debate among car designers across the globe.

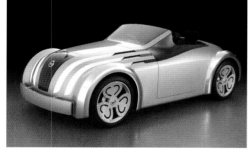

Nissan Pathfinder

Engine	4.0 V6
Power	186 kW (250 bhp)
Torque	366 Nm (270 lb. ft.)
Gearbox	5-speed automatic
Installation	Front-engined / all-wheel drive
Front suspension	Double wishbone
Rear suspension	Double wishbone
Brakes front/rear	Discs / discs
Front tyres	265 / 65R17
Rear tyres	265 / 65R17
Length	4766 mm (187.6 in.)
Width	1849 mm (72.8 in.)
Height	1775 mm (69.9 in.)
Wheelbase	2850 mm (112.2 in.)

The Pathfinder was first introduced in 1986 and at that time was Nissan's only SUV in North America. The family has grown and now includes the Pathfinder, the Xterra, the Murano and the Pathfinder Armada. The new Pathfinder is larger and more powerful than the outgoing model, and now comes with a third row of seats, so it can compete squarely with the best-selling SUV in North America, the Ford Explorer. Nevertheless, Ford will probably claim that its V8-powered SUV can still out-run the V6 Nissan in the power stakes.

The new Pathfinder follows the same design theme of previous models. It comes with a large power bulge on the bonnet, square headlamps, and grille bars that follow the theme of all new Nissan trucks. There are large, integrated, semicircular wing flares, and the angled C-pillars (a signature feature for Nissan SUVs) come complete with high-mounted rear door handles. The integrated roof rack is new, as is the rear tailgate design, which has a flip-up rear glass hatch opening like a Range Rover. For those who want personalization, there are optional side running boards, heated outside mirrors and a power slide/tilt sunroof.

The current Pathfinder has had a loyal following for years, so a larger, more powerful version that has been designed since canny Renault took control of drifting Nissan should have a decent chance of winning friends in this hotly contested segment, one that includes an ever-growing group of rival SUVs, including the recently redesigned Dodge Durango, the Chevrolet Trailblazer and the Ford Freestyle.

Nissan Qashqai

Installation	Front-engined / four-wheel drive
Brakes front/rear	Discs / discs
Length	4310 mm (169.7 in.)
Width	1860 mm (73.2 in.)
Height	1570 mm (61.8 in.)
Wheelbase	2650 mm (104.3 in.)

Named after a desert-dwelling nomadic tribe living near the Zagros Mountains in south-western Iran, Qashqai is envisaged by Nissan as an 'urban nomad'. It is aimed at young professional people who enjoy living and working in the city during the week but who want to escape at the weekend. Significantly, it is the first project to emerge from the newly established Nissan Design Europe (NDE) studio in west London, a 'think tank' dedicated to developing advanced designs for European markets.

As a crossover vehicle, it combines a sporting hatchback body on a 4x4 platform. It has a striking coupé-like roof, a high waistline and an aerofoil shape to the side glass. The surfaces and lines fight spiritedly with one another, causing plenty of visible tension and attitude. The rear lights run up and over to the tailgate to accentuate the car's tall stance. At the front, the headlamp clusters incorporate the turn indicators and fog lamps, as well as the LED headlamps themselves, but are covered in a newly developed 'clear-ink' paint that matches the car's body colour but becomes invisible once a light is shone through it.

One interior design feature pays homage to the studio where it was designed. NDE's home in London's Paddington is a building called the Rotunda, constructed in 1966 and originally a railway maintenance depot. Some of the graffiti covering the building was retained during its renovation, and this inspired the motif for the slash of patterned colour that rings the passenger's side of the cockpit. It's an unusual way, perhaps, to capture the wit of London's own youthful urban nomads.

Nissan Redigo

Engine	1.4 in-line 4
Gearbox	CVT
Installation	Four-wheel drive
Front tyres	195/60R17
Rear tyres	195/60R17
Length	3830 mm (150.8 in.)
Width	1695 mm (66.7 in.)
Height	1660 mm (65.4 in.)
Wheelbase	2465 mm (97 in.)

The Nissan Redigo is a cheeky targa-top coupé finished in garish green for the show car. Its body has taut vertical sides with a prominent waist-level 'shelf' that runs completely around the body, making it look a bit like a boat; there are also corresponding sculpted recesses housing aluminium strips at the side that look distinctly like waterline marks. At the front, the stripy vertical LED headlamps look futuristic and echo the side strips. There is a large retractable glass roof that opens towards the centre spine and, when it and the side windows are retracted, a genuine feeling of openness is created. Overall, the design is fussy for a car made up largely of simple lozenge shapes outside and in, formed by true radii and straight lines.

Two lozenge-like instrument panels sit on the dash, one in front of the driver and the other in front of the passenger; the driver's shows such vital information as speed and various in-car warning lights, while the passenger's display is moveable and conveys navigation and entertainment information. The doors, seats and floor use water-resistant materials, sensible for a 'ready-go' fun car likely to find itself out in all weathers. The door trim and head restraints are covered in a soft, yet glossy, polyurethane material, while cheerful-looking mesh material covers the seat backs.

The design theme of Redigo is articulated strongly, no doubt about it: but there would be a very limited market indeed for such a car.

Nissan Serenity

Gearbox	CVT
Installation	Front-engined / front-wheel drive
Front tyres	225 / 45R19
Rear tyres	225 / 45R19
Length	4700 mm (185 in.)
Width	1780 mm (70 in.)
Height	1550 mm (61 in.)
Wheelbase	2900 mm (114.2 in.)

As the name implies, the overall design is built around 'serenity' – a key characteristic of Japanese culture. It's likely to be a crowd-puller at home, but is far too esoteric for international markets. So enjoy the Serenity here because you probably won't see it again.

The overall proportion is of a monospace complete with a gently rising roofline that drops slightly at the rear to create an arc. The design language of many of the body features is angular by comparison and appears edgy and at odds with the rest of it – hardly creating a feeling of serenity.

The car's face combines large flat forms with strong lamp and grille features that are extremely detailed, in an attempt to echo Japanese latticework. This intrinsic detail cleverly accentuates the calmness of the flat, uninterrupted surfaces. Along the side, the windows give a feeble representation of a folding Japanese fan, but end up looking plain awkward. At the rear, the lamps are extremely large, and graphically striking when lit.

There is a much more relaxed feel to the interior, you'll be pleased to hear. The two-tone interior trim combines 'cherry beige' with a subdued dark grey to create a largely serene ambience. There is a wide dashboard with gentle flowing forms and a digital read-out that presents information in a soft yellow glow.

The 'City Browser' is a new technical information feature. This picks up live information – special offers transmitted from shops en route or historical information on nearby landmarks, for example – to keep Serenity travellers informed with local text and voice information. Or, as most legislators would have it, cause a distraction that could lead to a crash – which wouldn't be that serene, either.

Opel/Vauxhall Astra

Design	Friedhelm Engler
Engine	2.0 in-line 4 turbo (1.4, 1.6 and 1.8 in-line 4, and 1.7 and 1.9 in-line 4 turbo-diesel, also offered)
Power	149 kW (200 bhp) @ 5600 rpm
Torque	250 Nm (184 lb. ft.) @ 1950–5600 rpm
Gearbox	5-speed manual
Installation	Front-engined/front-wheel drive
Front suspension	MacPherson strut
Brakes front/rear	Discs/discs
Front tyres	215/40ZR17
Rear tyres	215/40ZR17
Length	4110 mm (161.8 in.)
Width	1709 mm (67.3 in.)
Height	1425 mm (56.1 in.)
Wheelbase	2606 mm (102.6 in.)
Kerb weight	1200 kg (2646 lb.)
0–100 km/h (62 mph)	7.5 sec
Top speed	240 km/h (150 mph)
Fuel consumption	8.9 l/100 km (31.7 mpg)

Opel (or Vauxhall, in the UK) has upgraded the Astra significantly for the 2004 model year. Not that it will make much impact, because its taut surfaces and straight feature lines make it look dated by comparison with rival models that already sell more (the Volkswagen Golf, say). We all know this is Opel's popular choice for the blue-collar worker, but General Motors' European division could still try to inject just a little more emotion into its surfaces.

The 'Njoy' equipment line adds the usual details to the Astra's interior and exterior, such as a chrome strip on the radiator grille, darkened tail lights and headlamps, body-coloured door handles, and attractive seven-spoke wheels with a flat profile. The interior has a leather steering wheel, chrome detailing, a dark-grey centre console and standard air-conditioning. Additional features of the 'Sport' level version include a sport chassis, a 20 mm (0.75 in.) lower body, sports seats in the front, a sporty leather steering wheel, ten-spoke alloy wheels and colour-keyed protective side mouldings. Customers opting for the top 'Elegance' trim also get electronic climate control, a leather-covered steering wheel with height adjustment, an in-car computer, burl-wood trim, cruise control and a windscreen rain sensor.

The fact is, though, even small cars today can offer this level of spec, so what would make you choose the Astra? That's difficult to see: the Astra appears to be a car that's scared to express an identity. It's all-round bland. Taut surfaces, gently rounded-off forms and unimaginative detailing make the whole package appear just a bit dull and old, which is a shame because the mechanicals are fairly good.

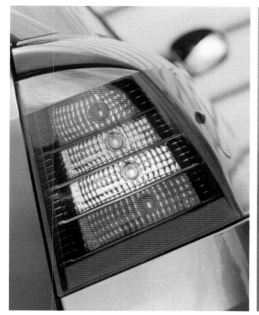

Opel Insignia

Design	Martin Smith
Engine	V8
Power	257 kW (344 bhp)
Installation	Front-engined / rear-wheel drive
Brakes front/rear	Discs / discs
Length	4803 mm (189 in.)
Width	1914 mm (75.4 in.)
Height	1414 mm (55.7 in.)
Wheelbase	2915 mm (114.8 in.)
Track front/rear	1666 / 1666 mm (65.6 / 65.6 in.)
0–100 km/h (62 mph)	< 6 sec
Top speed	250 km / h (155 mph) limited

The Insignia looks like it means business, with its boldly slatted front grille jutting pugnaciously outward to the lower bumper and through the lamps. It's a big car and it looks it. The proportion is of a coupé, with a long, V-shaped bonnet and sweeping A-pillars that lead on to a roof that slopes gently rearward over the combined rear screen/hatchback. From the side, strong shoulder lines grow from the front and the rear wings, emphasizing an inbuilt strength. Chrome trim plastered on above and below the doors signifies linear motion even when the Insignia is stationary, and there's no B-pillar to spoil the linear flow.

The rear doors use what, in the car industry, is termed a 'pantograph' mechanism. Like a sliding side door on a delivery van, the doors move parallel to the body rather than swinging outward. So the door is kept close to the body when open, making access much easier in car parks and other tight situations; but, unlike a typical sliding door, the stylist has more freedom to be adventurous because no ugly slider rails are needed on the door or main body carcass.

Inside, tobacco-brown leather contrasts with turquoise decorative seams, and inlays made of dark Macassar ebony wood, with darker brown, high-gloss lacquer surfaces, combine with satin-finished aluminium. All this is illuminated by indirect blue and green light emitted mysteriously by diodes located in concealed slots in the doors and ceiling. Strangely, the instrument pack dials are positioned in front of the needles; the numerals are visible as the needle moves past them because the transparent dials use LEDs; interesting, if crazily over-elaborate.

Opel Trixx

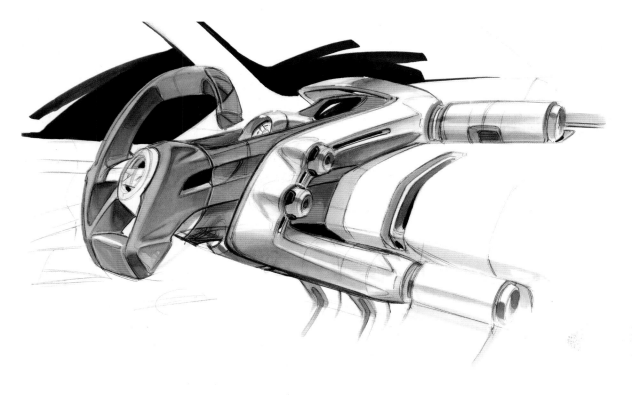

Engine	1.3 in-line 4 diesel
Power	52 kW (70 bhp)
Installation	Front-engined / front-wheel drive
Front tyres	175 / 55R17
Rear tyres	175 / 55R17
Length	3040 mm (119.7 in.)
Width	1660 mm (65.4 in.)
Height	1570 mm (61.8 in.)
Wheelbase	1940 mm (76.4 in.)
Track front/rear	1510/1510 mm (59.4 / 59.4 in.)
0–100 km/h (62 mph)	13.2 sec
Top speed	170 km/h (106 mph)
Fuel consumption	3.9 l / 100 km (72 mpg)

The Trixx is essentially a packaging study to discover how to get the most space from a small car 3 metres (10 ft.) long. The wheels are positioned right at the corners, although they are not pushed quite to the body's extremities as found in the Smart Fortwo (the new name for the Smart City Coupé), for example. The A-pillar is positioned far forward, allowing the Trixx to carry up to three adults and a child or, by rearranging the cabin, transform itself into a single-seater cargo-carrier with space for bulky loads. The inflatable passenger seat for a third adult is an interesting idea.

The Trixx adopts regular Opel design language, including the bold shoulder lines, short overhangs, prominent wheel arch lips and a centre-line crease in the bonnet. It is designed for people living in cities who need a compact car that offers agile handling, good visibility and ease of parking in tight spaces. The ingenious doors are electrically powered and swing out and forward on large hinges.

Inside, the aluminium cockpit and instruments have a 3D effect, especially the speedometer designed in the style of an American car of the 1950s, which is deeply recessed. The navigation system and main instrument cluster are mounted high up on the aluminium instrument panel. As on a motorcycle, all the instrumentation is directly in the field of view; in fact, two instruments move with the steering wheel as it is adjusted.

Trixx could evolve into the new Opel Corsa, although it would probably lose some of its radical touches. However, it's more likely that the Corsa replacement will be an altogether larger car while a sanitized descendant of the Trixx will become Opel's new A-segment offering.

Peugeot 407

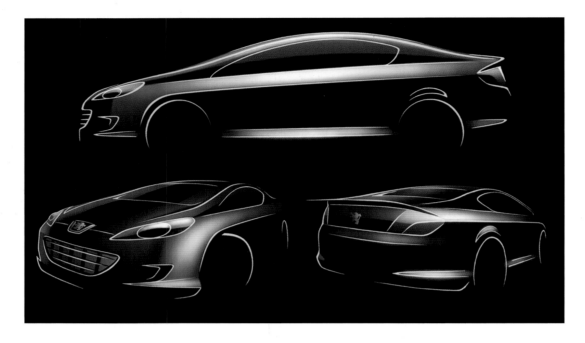

Engine	3.0 V6 (1.8, 2.0 and 2.2 in-line 4, and 1.6 and 2.0 in-line 4 diesel, also offered)
Power	157 kW (211 bhp)
Torque	296 Nm (218 lb. ft.)
Gearbox	6-speed automatic
Installation	Front-engined/front-wheel drive
Front suspension	Double wishbone
Rear suspension	Multi-link
Brakes front/rear	Discs/discs
Front tyres	215/55R17
Rear tyres	215/55R17
Length	4676 mm (184.1 in.)
Width	1811 mm (71.3 in.)
Height	1445 mm (56.9 in.)
Wheelbase	2725 mm (107.3 in.)
Track front/rear	1560/1526 mm (61.4/60.1 in.)
Kerb weight	1660 kg (3660 lb.)
0–100 km/h (62 mph)	8.4 sec
Top speed	235 km/h (146 mph)
Fuel consumption	9.8 l/100 km (28.8 mpg)
CO$_2$ emissions	233 g/km

The new 407 is much more dynamic and has a more upmarket feel than the 406 it supplants in Peugeot's catalogue. At the front, the large, slatted open-mouth grille draws air into the radiator and makes the car look fast, as if it wants to grab as much oxygen as it possibly can to sprint ahead. Large headlamps sweep back around the bumper and create a highly tapered front end in plan view; nevertheless, it appears plasticky and lightweight due to the obstinately three-dimensional design, especially compared to several stronger-looking German models that long-term customers trust.

A V-shaped ridge runs from the front of the bonnet up into the A-pillars, creating a strong reinforcement. But this is cosmetic because the important structure lies well below it, alongside the engine. Around the car, low down, is a small outward-facing lip that gives a sporty look and lowers the visual centre of gravity to make the 407 appear extra solid. Flared wheel arches boost the sporty feel.

It is at the rear that the 407 has been most successfully resolved. The boot surface gently tails off to a small lip spoiler, while the strength of the deep, rectangular rear lamp clusters is evident – at last giving a more upmarket look.

Peugeot is aiming to build on its reputation for excellent driving manners, so the 407 features double-wishbone front suspension, which offers greater stability and steering precision over more standard MacPherson struts.

A car of contrasts, the 407 will probably sell well, for Peugeot is an adept marketeer of everything it produces. But this is no Audi.

Peugeot 407 Elixir

Design	Gerard Welter
Engine	2.7 in-line 6 diesel
Power	148 kW (199 bhp)
Torque	440 Nm (324 lb. ft.)
Front suspension	Double wishbone
Rear suspension	Double wishbone
Brakes front/rear	Discs / discs
Length	4734 mm (186.4 in.)
Width	1920 mm (75.6 in.)
Height	1400 mm (55 in.)
Wheelbase	2725 mm (107.3 in.)
Track front/rear	1646 / 1684 mm (64.8 / 66.3 in.)

In its elegant, low-slung proportions, the 407 Elixir inadvertently pays homage to the Citroën C-Airdream concept launched a year earlier. The Elixir has an aerodynamic fastback proportion accentuated by long headlamps, a fast windscreen and that fastback roofline. The front looks more powerful than the C-Airdream's did, with the wide black grille dominating and giving a more purposeful appearance. Feature lines in the front bumper, sills and doors add to the sporty dimension of a car clearly proud of its enthusiast-pleasing Tiptronic transmission and double-wishbone suspension.

Inside, all occupants – the rear two included – get individual bucket seats for more comfort and adjustment. The Elixir also comes with 'dual zone' air-conditioning and a satellite navigation system complete with a 7 in. colour screen. The interior materials use pale colours to make the most of the light that streams in through the large glass roof. There's aluminium trim too, supposedly to highlight the Elixir's sportiness, but this stuff has become clichéd and ubiquitous – it really doesn't match the elegance of the exterior style.

This new concept has earned Peugeot much praise from the industry: its design somehow captures the elegance of a bygone era yet with built-in new technologies, to create something exciting for now. It's to be hoped that either Peugeot or Citroën will be convinced there's a market for this kind of model because this is a piece of carefully crafted French design. And that's not something you could level at either the Peugeot 607 or the Citroën C5.

Pontiac G6

Design	Jeff Perkins
Engine	3.5 V6 (2.4 in-line 4 also offered)
Power	149 kW (200 bhp) @ 5200 rpm
Torque	299 Nm (220 lb. ft.) @ 4400 rpm
Gearbox	4-speed automatic
Installation	Front-engined / front-wheel drive
Front suspension	MacPherson strut
Rear suspension	Multi-link
Brakes front/rear	Discs/discs
Front tyres	P225/50R17
Rear tyres	P225/50R17
Length	4802 mm (189 in.)
Width	1749 mm (68.9 in.)
Height	1450 mm (57 in.)
Wheelbase	2852 mm (112.3 in.)
Track front/rear	1519/1534 mm (59.8/60.4 in.)
Kerb weight	1555 kg (61.2 lb.)

Pontiac has already launched the G6 saloon, and promises that a two-plus-two coupé and convertible will shortly follow. The saloon G6 has a particularly long wheelbase, which is made obvious by the large doors and the fact that the rear wheel arch does not encroach into the rear-door shutline. This long wheelbase has the effect of making the cabin appear larger and the bonnet and boot lid appear shorter. Indeed, the car has relatively generous legroom, but only average luggage capacity; you can be assured that market research into real-life usage means this ratio probably suits the target audience just fine.

The front-end design is very bold. There are a large dark-meshed grille, raised projector headlamps and wide slatted air intakes that traverse the lower bumper. The bonnet rises sharply to the base of the windscreen, where the parked windscreen wipers are unconcealed – not typical of a luxury car because they usually produce an increase in wind noise. To improve sideways visibility, the waistline drops slightly at the door mirror and then gradually rises as it travels along to the C-pillar. This creates a curve that appears, oddly, like an unresolved packaging compromise, rather than a desirable aspect intentionally created by the designer.

The design at the rear is strong and sporty, with a small lip spoiler, an angular boot lid and rear lamps that wrap forward to form an arrow shape on the rear wings. The interior is dark with metal accents to give it a quality feel, but a circular theme throughout is a touch overwhelming.

Pontiac's G6 is a spacious car and a concerted effort has been made to give it a visible tension. That should make it a talking point on American driveways more used to the blandness or safeness (depending on your standpoint) of the Toyota Camry.

Pontiac Solstice

Design	Franz Von Holzhausen and Vicki Vlachakis
Engine	2.4 in-line 4
Power	127 kW (170 bhp) @ 6400 rpm
Torque	230 Nm (170 lb. ft.) @ 4400 rpm
Gearbox	5-speed manual
Installation	Front-engined / rear-wheel drive
Front suspension	Short and long arm
Rear suspension	Short and long arm
Brakes front/rear	Discs/discs
Front tyres	245/45R18
Rear tyres	245/45R18
Length	3994 mm (157.2 in.)
Width	1819 mm (71.6 in.)
Height	1274 mm (50.2 in.)
Wheelbase	2415 mm (95 in.)
Track front/rear	1537/1555 mm (60.5/61.2 in.)
Kerb weight	1300 kg (2866 lb.)

The Solstice roadster got a fantastic reaction from press and public alike when it was first shown as a concept at the 2002 Detroit show. With curvaceous and pulse-racing styling, it seemed to promise thrilling open-air driving. That old showman Bob Lutz, president of GM, responded quickly to this positive reaction; he personally ensured that the Solstice reached production in record time. To do this, Pontiac has adopted GM's Kappa platform architecture, which, being constructed from hydro-formed rails, has a high stiffness particularly suitable to the ride and handling demands of convertibles.

The production model deviates only a little from the concept, and includes all the crucial, crowd-pleasing elements such as the rear-wheel drive, the two-seater layout, the reverse-hinged clamshell bonnet and the bulges behind the headrests that hark back to sports cars of the past.

The front and rear bumpers are slightly longer on the production model for improved crash performance, but overall the proportion and minimalism are thankfully unspoilt. This is overtly a driver's car, and therefore the body surfaces are designed to encircle its occupants, the wheels and the engine – in fact, all that is necessary for back-to-basics fun driving. The interior is totally driver-oriented, with a dark-grey console that wraps over to encapsulate the instruments and driver controls, including the sporty, stubby gearstick.

Here is a dedicated sports car that hides its shared components from GM's parts bin brilliantly. The purity and function of the Solstice is unsullied. Pontiac has made a giant leap forward with this car in design and image terms, and created what is certain to be a future classic.

Renault BeBop

Design	Patrick le Quément
Engine	2.0 in-line 4 (1.6 also offered)
Power	168 kW (225 bhp)
Torque	300 Nm (221 lb. ft.)
Gearbox	6-speed manual
Installation	Front-engined / four-wheel drive
Brakes front/rear	Discs / discs
Front tyres	225 x 770 / R540 PAX
Rear tyres	225 x 770 / R540 PAX
Length	4040 mm (159 in.)
Width	1770 mm (69.7 in.)
Height	1550 mm (61 in.)
Wheelbase	2570 mm (101.2 in.)
Track front/rear	1550 / 1550 mm (61 / 61 in.)
Kerb weight	1300 kg (2866 lb.)

It's not often you see such a friendly-looking design-led product as this one. Renault has been constantly challenging itself to re-evaluate the side profile of popular car design over the last few years; that's clear from various models featured in previous editions of *The Car Design Yearbook*. This latest concept, the BeBop (not, of course, to be confused with the 1989 Ghia Bebop, a Ford Fiesta-based concept pickup) is a compact MPV with rounded forms. There are two versions, a base SUV and a RenaultSport version, demonstrating that Renault is still committed to building the competition-oriented sub-brand in its own right.

From the side, the most dramatic feature is the pure teardrop window-glass shape. Okay, so this completely ignores how you might drop the glass into the front door when opening the window, but never mind. The glass above the waistline is all darkly tinted, contrasting with the bright paintwork of the body. The rear is quite planar, slightly curved in plan and broken by a sharp feature line that leads over the side glass.

The interior is quite minimal yet very playful and youthful in its design language, with what Renault terms 'touch design' controls. The choice of colours (occupying a spectrum between warm grey and tan) and materials (tough yet cosseting) are typically 'Renault-esque', but the burnt-red on the dashboard gives a warm and fun appearance.

This concept is too big a jump even for so relatively adventurous a company as Renault to risk putting into production. Still, it demonstrates exciting ideas that will slowly become more acceptable to the buying public; and then, production viability will be achievable.

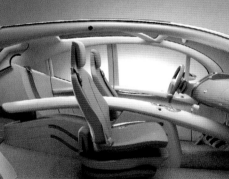

Renault Modus

Design	Patrick le Quément
Engine	1.6 in-line 4
Power	85 kW (115 bhp)
Installation	Front-engined / front-wheel drive
Length	3792 mm (149.3 in.)
Height	1589 mm (62.6 in.)

Modus is a concept that is virtually production-ready, even, some say, down to its name. It's a mini-MPV in the mould of the Opel Meriva that will sit very comfortably between the Twingo and the Scenic as part of Renault's passengers-first range that stretches up to the Espace.

There are specific playful features that help give Modus its cheerful look. When looking at a car, we (humans) instinctively pick up on features that would correspond to cheeriness on another person. This translates, in car terms, to our feeling well-disposed towards design that is warm and welcoming, and this the Modus achieves in spades. From the front, there are large, eye-like arched headlamps with small central pupil reflectors, and the lower grille in the bumper curves upward at the ends in a grinning manner.

The high roofline creates a large windscreen and side windows, which along with the glass roof allow light to flood the interior and give excellent all-round visibility. Along the side a key feature line that runs horizontally through the door handles deliberately sweeps upward towards the A-pillar. The effect this has is to remove some of the lateral movement and instead give a more attractive poise when Modus is static.

The interior is spacious owing to the one-box shape. An innovative new upholstery technique uses photographic printing to print a landscape motif on to the fabric. On the dashboard the controls are arranged using circular themes and have a youthful look to them.

If Renault decides to productionize the Modus then this will sit nicely in the sub-Scenic segment, and is sure to be a popular choice with European young families.

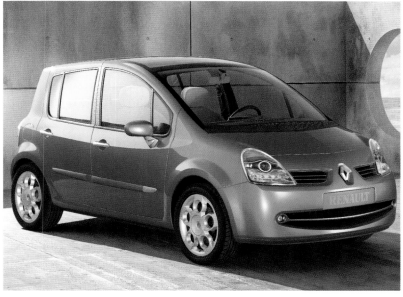

Renault Trafic Deck'up

This radical rethink of the Renault Trafic van – a commercial vehicle unveiled in 2000 that is still the most distinctive in its class – targets outdoor leisure and adventure markets. From the front, it uses the existing Trafic front-end design, but that is where the commonality stops. Dramatic saw-toothed side windows are framed in the silver bodywork, while the rear pickup area and lower body are visually separated using titanium grey. The driver's side has two conventionally opening doors, while the passenger side features no centre pillar so the rear door is rear-hinged to facilitate easier access.

The pickup section can be annexed from the passenger compartment by translucent glass shutters that slide away into the ceiling of the double cab. The small rear pickup area comes complete with protective roof bars and the interior has seating that can be configured so that rear passenger seats can swivel right round to face the deck area. When designing the Deck'up, Renault had the specific target market of safari photojournalists in mind! Inside there is a high centre console, with in-built storage, which can slide from the front to the rear of the vehicle.

The Deck'up is a very angular design emitting a reduced aura of utility as a result; it doesn't offer much space in the utility pickup area so it's bewildering to think what the Deck'up offers over, say, a more spacious Land Rover Freelander or many other small pickups with a crew cab. But full marks for creating something quite different.

Design	Patrick le Quément
Engine	2.5 in-line 4 diesel
Power	100 kW (135 bhp)
Gearbox	6-speed manual
Installation	Front-engined / front-wheel drive
Brakes front/rear	Discs / discs
Front tyres	255 / 55R20
Rear tyres	255 / 55R20
Length	4600 mm (181.1 in.)
Width	1925 mm (75.8 in.)
Height	2085 mm (82.1 in.)
Wheelbase	3020 mm (118.9 in.)

Renault Wind

Design	Patrick le Quément
Engine	2.0 in-line 4
Power	101 kW (136 bhp)
Torque	191 Nm (140 lb. ft.)
Gearbox	6-speed manual
Installation	Front-engined / front-wheel drive
Front tyres	245 / 35ZR19
Rear tyres	245 / 35ZR19
Length	3870 mm (152.4 in.)

A compact three-seater roadster, the Wind is a much more practical idea than Renault's last roadster. That was the Renault Spider, launched with a wind deflector instead of a windscreen, meaning that driver and passenger had to don eye protection (goggles at the very least) for safety. Amazingly, it was a production car and not just a showpiece, manufactured by Renault's now disbanded sports car division, Alpine.

The Wind sports gently flowing surfaces that hug the wheels and droop at the doors, interrupted by well-defined creases to sharpen key features such as the wheel arches and bonnet air intake. The headlamps and tail lamps are both flush-mounted to the body at an acute angle, giving the whole car movement even when it's motionless.

The Wind is short but has a long bonnet and a tall and panoramically curved windscreen that demonstrates that here is a fun motoring roadster and not some aerodynamic speed machine. The car's dynamics are enhanced by two distinctive lines that rise sharply, one below and the other above the door, to create a wedge-like shape, and rebalance visual interest in what would otherwise be a plain side view.

The cockpit naturally cocoons the driver by using dramatic, flowing, wave-like surfaces, and is typical of good classic roadster design. Tobacco-coloured pleated-leather seats are fixed and moulded with the centre console, while instrumentation is minimal and uses anodized finishes. Renault's 'touch design' philosophy, which puts the emphasis on ergonomics, simplicity and clarity, is well executed here.

This is more excellent design from Renault, which, true sports car lovers must fervently hope, could become a production reality in a couple of years.

Rinspeed Splash

Engine	0.75 2 cylinder
Power	104 kW (140 bhp) @ 7000 rpm
Torque	150 Nm (110 lb. ft.) @ 3500 rpm
Installation	Rear-engined / rear-wheel drive
Front suspension	Double wishbone
Rear suspension	Double wishbone
Brakes front/rear	Discs / discs
Front tyres	215 / 35R17
Rear tyres	225 / 35R18
Length	3760 mm (148 in.)
Width	1865 mm (73.4 in.)
Height	1230 mm (48.4 in.)
Wheelbase	2345 mm (92.3 in.)
Track front/rear	1600 / 1600 mm (63 / 63 in.)
Kerb weight	825 kg (1819 lb.)
0–100 km/h (62 mph)	5.9 sec
Top speed	200 / 80 km/h (125 / 50 mph) on land / in water

Rinspeed is a Swiss design company that has produced a parade of whacky concepts in the past. This is its tenth such vehicle, and it is not only a high-performance sports car but also an amphibious vehicle with an integrated hydrofoil system that enables it to 'fly' at about 60 cm (24 in.) above the water surface – high enough for the wheels to clear the wet stuff – at a speed of 80 km/h (50 mph).

The Splash is obviously a feat of engineering, but the styling is constrained by the fact that it carries 'marine architecture' functions that require it to have a narrowing front end. In fact, the styling compromise is mainly made because the Splash was schemed on a tight budget and must use donor parts from other cars. From the rear, it resembles an ambitious but still home-built sports car, whereas at the front the wheel arches look puny compared to the body's other chunky contours.

In transforming for the water, the rear panel flips up to reveal a propeller that is lowered to its correct aquatic position directly from the cockpit. The Formula 1-style rear spoiler rotates down at the rear, and on the left and right are two hydrofoils integrated into the outside skin. These rotate down before unfolding into their lifting V shape.

Inside, waterproof plastics naturally abound, and a series of chrome-plated switches rams home the Splash's groundbreaking (maybe that should also be waterbreaking) technology.

Rolls-Royce 100EX

The 100EX is the first concept car from Rolls-Royce since BMW became custodian of the marque in 1998. Indeed, it is the only Rolls concept, in the accepted use of the term, in the marque's hundred-year history. And furthermore, you can forget cold, damp England: the design team was based in southern California, at the BMW Group's Designworks studio, and took much inspiration from luxury yachts.

Based on an aluminium spaceframe structure, this open-top, four-seat, two-door drophead (convertible) was presented to celebrate Rolls-Royce's centenary, which fell in May 2004. Rolls-Royce has termed this an 'experimental' model as a satisfying historical tie-in; mostly in pre-war years, a series of cars was given an EX tag to signify that they were fully functioning prototypes, as this is supposed to be, rather than simply styling models.

The world-famous chrome grille is recessed within the front end and slightly reclines into the bonnet. The two-tone paintwork separates along the bonnet feature line, the lighter, polished-aluminium colour accentuating the power of the V16 engine below. From the dark-blue-painted side, the waistline profile rises as it passes the rear wheels and drops towards the rear. This styling stance is calculated to complement the Rolls-Royce tradition of 'waftability' – the sense of whisking passengers swiftly to high speed in a relaxed manner. To emphasize the body lines, a polished-aluminium waist rail encircles the passenger compartment.

Inside is a strong nautical theme. The interior wood veneer is figured mahogany, with upholstery in rich Dark Curzon leather, while the flooring features the same bleached-teak decking as the tonneau cover for the folded hood. Bleached-teak decking extends across the boot floor, providing a table-like surface accessed through a split boot lid with a drop-down lower platform.

There is no plan to produce the 100EX as a series model, but it is certainly more elegant than the recently launched Phantom saloon. What Sir Henry Royce would think of such ostentatiousness, in both cars, is anyone's guess.

Design	Ian Cameron
Engine	9.0 V16
Gearbox	6-speed automatic
Installation	Front-engined / rear-wheel drive
Brakes front/rear	Discs / discs
Front tyres	255 / 50R21
Rear tyres	285 / 45R21
Length	5669 mm (223.2 in.)
Width	1990 mm (78.3 in.)
Height	1561 mm (61.5 in.)
Wheelbase	3470 mm (136.6 in.)

Saab 9-2X

Design	Michael Mauer
Engine	2.5 in-line flat 4 (2.0 also offered)
Power	169 kW (227 bhp) @ 6000 rpm
Torque	294 Nm (217 lb. ft.) @ 4000 rpm
Gearbox	5-speed manual
Installation	Front-engined/four-wheel drive
Brakes front/rear	Discs/discs
Length	4460 mm (175.6 in.)
Wheelbase	2525 mm (99.4 in.)
Kerb weight	1400 kg (3086 lb.)

The 9-2X is Saab's latest new product and is in the vanguard of its biggest new-model development programme ever. The 9-2X targets a younger customer than usual for the Swedish company, so Saab has opted for a strong and dynamic character in its design, with more of a dash of aggression than the rest of the line-up.

However, all is not as it seems. Despite a distinctively Saab nose treatment, the car's visual pugnaciousness comes from the fact that it is really a Subaru Impreza five-door given a Swedish makeover. This outwardly unlikely amalgam is because General Motors – owner of Saab and a major stakeholder in Subaru – spotted the match-making possibility. It also gives Saab a new model in a new market at a fraction of the normal development cost.

The Impreza's pumped-up wheel arches and flared sills showcase the chunky ten-spoke wheels that are the delivery conduits of the four-wheel-drive drivetrain. The wrap-around rear window is another strong feature, while the 'hockey stick'-shape of the steeply raked C-pillar chimes in happily with the looks of Saab's bigger 9-5 estate.

The Saab quotient centres around the curvaceous front with its integrated three-hole grille and the horizontal emphasis of the headlamps that wrap around into the sides of the car. There's a gaping, macho air intake in the lower bumper, and a corresponding air scoop in the bonnet. Inside, a distinctive black, cream and titanium colour scheme appears sporty, but will date quickly.

The 9-2X is, initially, for sale in the United States and Canada, so that Saab can get to grips with the marketing issues of selling a car that it hasn't really designed itself. But Subaru has a great reputation for customer satisfaction and driving dynamics, so it should be a happy union – and a strong player in the 'premium sport compact' segment, where the Audi A3 is a benchmark.

Saab 9-3 Sport-Hatch

Design	Michael Mauer
Engine	2.0 in-line 4
Power	184 kW (247 bhp) @ 5500 rpm
Torque	350 Nm (258 lb. ft.) @ 2500 rpm
Gearbox	5-speed automatic
Installation	Front-engined / front-wheel drive
Front suspension	MacPherson strut
Rear suspension	Multi-link
Brakes front/rear	Discs / discs
Front tyres	245 / 40R20
Rear tyres	245 / 40R20
Length	4659 mm (183.4 in.)
Width	1801 mm (70.9 in.)
Height	1547 mm (60.9 in.)
Wheelbase	2700 mm (106.3 in.)
Track front/rear	1580 / 1566 mm (62.2 / 61.7 in.)
Kerb weight	1580 kg (3483 lb.)
0–100 km/h (62 mph)	7.1 sec
Top speed	250 km/h (155 mph) limited

The Saab 9-3 Sport-Hatch concept is, in essence, a sporty estate that carries forward much of the design language of the Saab 9-3X, a previous Saab concept, launched in 2002, that fused a hatchback and an estate with some light off-road capability.

Styling cues on the Sport-Hatch taken from the 9-3X include most of the rear-end treatment, with the relatively short overhang, the steeply raked rear screen and light assemblies, and the uninterrupted shape of the side-window glazing with disguised door pillars. The headlamps are bluntly rectangular, actually a fairly rare feature today – even the new VW Golf, known (lauded, even) for its conservatism, has its lamps cut into the bonnet. The beauty of the 9-3 comes from the purposeful forms allied to a sporty stance and some accomplished architectural detail – such as those statuesque rear lamps.

Saab has a massive challenge on its hands. With annual production at around 140,000 cars, it's a mid-size player competing in a mid-priced market. It needs to push upmarket – always extremely hard work – or increase market share … or cut costs by parts-sharing with other products in the General Motors group to stem further losses. So which is it to be with the slightly underwhelming Sport-Hatch? A production version is widely tipped to be on sale by the end of 2004, so it won't be long before we find out.

This is a generalization, but Saab buyers are often people who appreciate good design. Architects and designers among them, they search out great alternative design with inbuilt quality and excellent functionality. To their eyes, Saab stands for alternative affordable quality cars. It's this uniqueness that makes it so desirable. If Saab has to doff its cap to GM too much, it risks making design compromises with future products that lack the expected design brand values. Luckily, Saab has a tradition of taking a painfully long time to get new cars to market, so there is still hope that its painstaking methodology will keep its precious character intact.

Saturn Curve

Design	Nicho Vardis
Engine	2.2 in-line 4
Gearbox	5-speed manual
Installation	Front-engined / rear-wheel drive
Front suspension	MacPherson strut
Rear suspension	Short and long arm
Brakes front/rear	Discs / discs
Front tyres	245 / 40R20
Rear tyres	245 / 45R20
Length	3975 mm (156.5 in.)
Width	1950 mm (76.8 in.)
Height	1247 mm (49 in.)
Wheelbase	2717 mm (107 in.)

Here is a new two-plus-two concept for the US-only mid-market marque with an uncharacteristically international flavour: it was designed at General Motors' advanced design centre based at Saab's HQ in Sweden, and turned into a reality by Pininfarina's craftsmen in Italy. It is based on GM's brand-new, high-stiffness Kappa platform, one that has also been used on the production Pontiac Solstice and the Chevrolet Nomad concept.

The body exterior has an interestingly athletic appearance, focusing on distinctive and muscular forms. It has a high waistline, pronounced wheel arches and a long horizontal bonnet. The roof architecture radiates a very European look, achieved by black pillars and a wrap-around canopy of glass – creating the illusion of a 'floating' roof panel. Design symmetry is always reassuring and draws the eye. A good example is the clamshell front-hinged bonnet and rear-hinged boot when they are both in the 'up' position. Nevertheless, arresting as this arrangement may look, it's impractical.

The interior evokes raw sports styling, with such features as the open gearshift gate and the analogue instruments. The blonde-wood centre console dominates the interior and encapsulates the engine instruments sitting below the charcoal-coloured leather, which has terracotta inserts to accent dashboard and upholstery. Lighting around the rear seats gives the interior a warm glow but also has a safety use; when the doors are opened, the orange-red lighting on the door panels acts as a warning light, eliminating the need for a reflector.

The Curve is designed to generate interest in the Saturn brand beyond the usual family car good sense. Thanks to using the Kappa platform, we could see something similar translate into production reality quite soon.

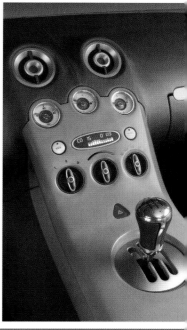

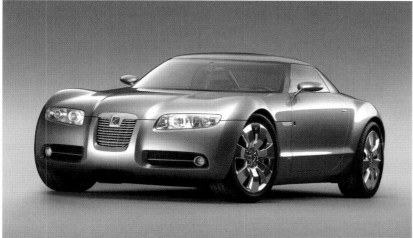

Scion tC

Design	Shunsaku Kodama
Engine	2.4 in-line 4
Power	119 kW (160 bhp) @ 5700 rpm
Torque	221 Nm (163 lb. ft.) @ 4000 rpm
Gearbox	5-speed manual
Installation	Front engined / front-wheel drive
Front suspension	MacPherson strut
Rear suspension	Double wishbone
Brakes front/rear	Discs / discs
Front tyres	P215 / 45R17
Rear tyres	P215 / 45R17
Length	4420 mm (174 in.)
Width	1755 mm (69.1 in.)
Height	1415 mm (55.7 in.)
Wheelbase	270 mm (106.3 in.)

Toyota's unfolding 'youthful brand', Scion, is getting to grips with the demands of its 'Generation Y' target customers (the post-'Generation X' market, we can only presume) with a new, much more exciting and expressive model than its underwhelming xA and xB. The new car is called tC and is a small coupé, which joined the xA and xB in the national Scion roll-out across the United States in the summer of 2004.

The tC is based on the European Avensis platform and comes with a 2.4 litre, 160 bhp engine. The tC is designed to be an affordable model, so there are no superfluous details on the body or the trim or inside the cabin. The car sits low with wheel arches that hug the sporty multi-spoked wheels. The body surfaces are closely wrapped around the engine and occupants. The waistline is high and the roof quickly drops at the rear, emphasizing that this car is designed around the driver.

Scion may claim that its very essence is visible in the tC, with its jolly amber instrument illumination. But almost every car these days incorporates metallic interior trim decoration like this one; it's very much a 'so what?' detail now. Car family 'DNA' should be most evident in exterior design language, in particular front-end design. Low-budget Scion lacks this, perhaps because its three current models are wrestling one another for the dominant Scion identity. When Toyota creates a more harmonious range, Scion stands a better chance of raising brand awareness and consequent sales.

Seat Altea

Design	Walter de' Silva
Engine	2.0 in-line 4 (1.6, and 1.9 and 2.0 diesel, also offered)
Power	110 kW (148 bhp) @ 6000 rpm
Torque	200 Nm (147 lb. ft.) @ 3500 rpm
Gearbox	6-speed Tiptronic
Installation	Front-engined/front-wheel drive
Front suspension	MacPherson strut
Rear suspension	Multi-link
Brakes front/rear	Discs/discs
Front tyres	245/35R19
Rear tyres	245/35R19
Length	4280 mm (168.5 in.)
Width	1770 mm (69.7 in.)
Height	1570 mm (61.8 in.)
Wheelbase	2578 mm (101.5 in.)
Track front/rear	1551/1532 mm (61/60.3 in.)
Kerb weight	1428 kg (3148 lb.)
0–100 km/h (62 mph)	9.6 sec
Top speed	206 km/h (128 mph)
Fuel consumption	7.7 l/100 km (36.7 mpg)
CO_2 emissions	201.6 g/km

The Altea is largely based on the Salsa concept, unveiled at the 2000 Geneva Motor Show. Offered as a concept at Frankfurt in 2003 and then unveiled in a production version at Geneva in 2004, this is a rare case of the production model following the almost identical concept very swiftly so that Seat can make itself look on the ball.

The Altea comes dripping with Latin spirit and has a distinctive look thanks to headlamp clusters with the look of cat's eyes. These are no ordinary headlamps either, because they feature a so-called variable iris system that uses a single gas-discharge bulb, and a radial-opening diaphragm, like the iris of an eye. When the diaphragm is closed, light from the bulb reflects only off the front surrounding reflector, resulting in a dipped beam. When the diaphragm is open, light also reflects off the rear reflector, producing a powerful high beam. Seat claims that fog lamps are unnecessary with this newly patented system.

The broad air vents beneath the grille give the 'face' a dynamic poise, beginning at the front spoiler, extending over the front wheel arch and continuing gradually downward to the rear wheel hub. The rear end features a broad hatchback and an outward positioning of the tail lights. At the top of the rear hatch the spoiler displays the third brake light and rear wiper, while a group of light-emitting diodes on the bumper houses the reverse lights and fog lamps.

Inside there are two main materials, the background warm-grey layer used on the dashboard, instrument panel dials, side panels and headlining, and unpolished aluminium on the steering wheel spokes, levers, ventilation nozzles, boot mouldings and switches. The door-panel design also echoes the silhouette of the exterior.

This genuinely fun Seat will offer strong competition to the Ford Fiesta, among other rivals. The Altea exudes vitality in a massive market sector often characterized by rather dull practicality.

Seat Cupra GT

Design	Walter de' Silva
Engine	3.0 V6
Power	373 kW (500 bhp)
Torque	600 Nm (452 lb. ft.) @ 5250 rpm
Gearbox	6-speed sequential
Installation	Mid-engined / rear-wheel drive
Front suspension	Double wishbone
Rear suspension	Double wishbone
Brakes front/rear	Discs / discs
Length	4562 mm (179.6 in.)
Width	2100 mm (82.7 in.)
Height	1190 mm (46.9 in.)
Wheelbase	2650 mm (104.3 in.)
Track front/rear	1843 / 1818 mm (72.6 / 71.6 in.)
Kerb weight	1100 kg (2425 lb.)
0–100 km/h (62 mph)	4.2 sec
Top speed	295 km/h (183 mph)

The premiere of the Seat Cupra GT at the Barcelona show was a very exciting spectacle for an event that doesn't normally attract new model launches.

The Cupra GT was obviously designed specifically for the racetrack; why else would Seat need a 500 bhp supercar? It's a great way to build excitement into the Seat brand, especially as the VW Group has accumulated so much supercar expertise recently in the Bugatti Veyron, the VW W12, the Lamborghini Murciélago and the new Audi Le Mans.

For those familiar with Seat's recent concept cars, it comes as no surprise that the Cupra GT inherits design lines from the Salsa and the sexy Tango, while also projecting the image of Seat's usually annoying motto 'auto emoción' – that is, expressive design and sportiness with an innovative character.

It has a short front overhang initiating a sinuous feature line that rises to define the edge of the head-lamps and the top of the wings and then sweeps rearward through the door in a similar way to the Tango concept. The skin is made from carbon fibre for ultimate stiffness and low weight. The doors are termed 'seagull wing' because of the way they open, their hinges located on the top of the pillar.

The huge wheels feature a single centre nut for faster tyre changes, while at the rear the big wings give a muscular look, and the titanium-coloured bumper is integrated into the rear end above the diffuser. The rear roof spoiler balances the downforce given by the front intake vents to help stabilize the car at speed. The two air-intake vents behind the doors cool the engine and feed the intercoolers.

This spectacular model should keep Seat's marketing department very happy in the short term, even though its grid debut seems but a distant possibility.

Skoda Octavia

Design	Dirk van Braeckel
Engine	1.8 in-line 4 turbo (1.4, 1.6 and 2.0 in-line 4, and 1.9 in-line 4 diesel, also offered)
Power	112 kW (150 bhp)
Torque	173 Nm (127 lb. ft.) @ 1950–5000 rpm
Gearbox	5-speed manual
Installation	Front-engined/all-wheel drive
Front suspension	MacPherson strut
Rear suspension	Torsion beam
Brakes front/rear	Discs/discs
0–100 km/h (62 mph)	7.9 sec
Top speed	235 km/h (146 mph)
Fuel consumption	8.1 l/100 km (35 mpg)

When the Octavia was unveiled in 1996, it single-handedly changed the public perception of Skoda, lifting it from the depressing gutter of Communist-era economy motoring to a position as a junior yet entirely competent relation of Volkswagen. It became widely known that Skoda would henceforth use Volkswagen platforms on which to base its new cars; this had an immediate and marked effect on the quality of its new models, to the extent that many pundits asked with some justification whether an equivalent VW (the Golf) was worth the premium demanded.

The replacement Octavia is designed by Dirk van Braeckel, and is likewise built in the Czech Republic at what is now a world-class production facility. It has clean lines that are contemporary and very sensible, giving it the appearance of a car driven within the laws of the land rather than something evocative and sporty that sees onlookers salivating in excitement. This is an understated design for people who want a quality car without any frills. The proportion is of a classic saloon adorned with crisp feature lines, a bold grille and large lamps at front and rear.

The previous Octavia achieved an outstanding accolade; it was voted Best Family Car by consumers in the 2003 JD Power Customer Satisfaction Index in Britain, so this new model has a lot to live up to. With traditional proportions and thrifty values, the new Octavia should remain the ultimate choice for people who own caravans.

Skoda Roomster

Design	Thomas Ingenlath
Length	4055 mm (159.6 in.)
Width	1843 mm (72.6 in.)
Height	1669 mm (65.7 in.)
Wheelbase	2710 mm (106.7 in.)

The Roomster is Skoda's vision for a compact family car for the future. The design is really quite extra-ordinary and makes a deliberate distinction between a wrap-around driving environment, with all-round vision, and a rear passenger space designed for a variety of functions, made possible in a relaxed and cheerful environment. From above, the Roomster is unusual, as both the outline of the sunroofs and the windscreen create the shape of an arrow. As with all current production Skodas, the Roomster places great emphasis on its monolithic structure: the entire body appears as one complete cast.

The Roomster introduces design elements that may appear on future Skodas. Such familiar details as the grille, with its simple, vertical ribbing, are newly interpreted, and the Roomster incorporates robust door columns that narrow as they move upward. Asymmetrical construction means there's a rear door only on the passenger side; it reaches high into the roof and has no cumbersome sill, so that access to the back seats is unimpeded and comfortable. Consequently, there are two different side views: the roofline on the driver's side is continuous along the car's length, while on the passenger side it rises in a curve.

The Roomster is only a design study but it presents a possible, and highly feasible, direction for Skoda. True, it's a keenly priced, solid brand these days, but there's always scope for owner Volkswagen to cut some passionate new cloth for its most conservative marque. Only the name is awful: either Skoda feels all the good ones have gone, or else it's a sideswipe at the Porsche Boxster.

Smart Forfour

Engine	1.5 in-line 4 (1.1 and 1.3 also offered)
Power	80 kW (107 bhp)
Torque	145 Nm (107 lb. ft.)
Gearbox	5-speed manual
Installation	Front-engined / front-wheel drive
Front suspension	MacPherson strut
Rear suspension	Compound crank axle
Brakes front/rear	Discs / discs
Front tyres	195 / 50R15
Rear tyres	195 / 50R15
Length	3752 mm (147.7 in.)
Width	1684 mm (66.3 in.)
Height	1450 mm (57.1 in.)
Wheelbase	2500 mm (98.4 in.)
Track front/rear	1460 / 1445 mm (57.5 / 56.9 in.)
Kerb weight	975 kg (2150 lb.)
0 – 100 km/h (62 mph)	10 sec
Top speed	190 km/h (118 mph)
Fuel consumption	6 l/100 km (47 mpg)

The Smart Forfour possesses the must-have appeal of a young car brand and is the first four-door, four-seater Smart – hence the no-nonsense name. The typical brand features remain, such as the visible Tridion (in Smart-speak) safety cell complete with its contrasting-colour concept. The proportions and design language of the car are typically Smart, evoking bold, simple, domestic-product design and rejecting the expected dimensions adopted by most five-door hatchbacks.

The Smart Forfour, complete with its 'smiley face', conveys a sense of *joie de vivre*. This friendly visage is characterized by its four individual, vertically mounted headlamps, positioned at an angle to each other above the air inlet. At the rear, the three-dimensional circular tail lamps are what we now know as typically Smart. There's no doubt, though, that in broadening its range into family cars, Smart is taking risks with its self-conscious rebelliousness: even its two-seater roadster, unleashed in 2002, looks radical and features an unusual rear-mounted engine.

As with other Smart models, the Pulse model line offers a full range of high-quality, sporty features, while the Passion caters to the highest comfort requirements. The Smart Forfour's Tridion safety cell is available in three colourways: silver, black or titanium. These three can then be combined with the body panels, which are available in ten typically lurid Smart colours.

The Forfour was developed in co-operation with Mitsubishi and shares a number of parts with Mitsubishi's own new Compact Car, including engines, rear axle, structural components in the car underbody, manual transmission and the emissions and fuel tank system.

Deliveries started in summer 2004 and for buyers with sportier aspirations there's a tempting list of Brabus-designed accessories to turn a Forfour into a pseudo street-racer.

Subaru B9 Scrambler

Subaru has a new chief designer, Andreas Zapatinas, who heads its Advanced Design Studio. Zapatinas is an ex-Alfa Romeo designer, which certainly goes a long way towards explaining the visually striking new face at Subaru. The B9 Scrambler, one of his first pieces of work, has a dominant grille in the shape of an aircraft fuselage, recalling Subaru's long-ago aircraft heritage, and is flanked by two separate grilles that vaguely echo aircraft wings. The air intakes in the lower bumper also have this shape and give the design a slightly retro look – not far removed from the BMW Z8 that, worryingly, was a commercial disaster despite its high price and James Bond movie marketing tie-in.

The B9 Scrambler looks low and streamlined, an effect amplified by two-tone paintwork that splits midway up the side of the car in a striking way, as if a large blue cloth has been draped over the upper body. The windscreen surround is a thin chrome strip that conveys lightness and agility to the upper body.

All previous Subarus have given most emphasis to their technical abilities; for a change, the styling gets equal billing here. The Scrambler comes with some off-road competence thanks to its all-wheel drive system and variable-height air suspension that features automatic self-levelling and a ride-height range of 150–200 mm (6–8 in.). Powering the Scrambler is a petrol-electric hybrid engine that uses an electric motor up to speeds of 80 km/h (50 mph), only turning over to the burning of fossil fuel when the charge drops below a certain level.

Subaru desperately needs a new modern identity. If anyone can create that, it's Zapatinas. Stay tuned.

Design	Andreas Zapatinas
Engine	Petrol-electric hybrid engine
Installation	Front-engined / all-wheel drive

Subaru Justy

Engine	1.5 in-line 4 (1.3, and 1.3 diesel, also offered)
Gearbox	5-speed manual
Installation	Front-engined /all-wheel drive
Front suspension	MacPherson strut
Rear suspension	Multi-link
Brakes front/rear	Discs /discs

At the heart of the Subaru brand lies excellent technology, most often centred around a sophisticated all-wheel-drive system. Beyond this technical inner force, however, Subaru has offered design that's been mediocre at best.

Now we are starting to see some progress and, in the Justy, based on the Suzuki Ignis (the latest move in a long-standing co-operative relationship between Subaru and Suzuki), we have a tough car with a purposeful stance. Bulging wheel arches hint at the off-road potential, although this will be relatively tame with only a maximum 1.5 litre powertrain. With only 170 mm (6.75 in.) of ground clearance, this is actually a crossover car for the city and occasional dirt-track driving, rather than for traversing rivers. The twin grilles at the front give the car real presence above and beyond its actual performance. The combination of square and round lamps adds a clever touch in separating the car-like upper body from the off-road lower body replete with all its trimmings.

The all-wheel drive gives traction in difficult driving conditions or on rough roads, and comes complete with a viscous coupling that enhances the torque split to maintain traction.

Inside there are also the usual benefits of this type of car, centred around the higher driving position for better visibility and easier access. The three-spoke steering wheel, gearshift knob and skirt have a sporty feel, while the instrument panel and information display impart luxury.

This car is what the disappointingly bland Ford Fusion should have turned out to be like, to avoid the slow-selling model it instantly became. The Subaru Justy has personality and deserves to do well.

Subaru Legacy and Outback

Design	Tetsuya Jirobo
Engine	3.0 flat 6 (2.0 and 2.5 flat 4 also offered)
Power	178 kW (241 bhp) @ 6600 rpm
Torque	297 Nm (219 lb. ft.) @ 4200 rpm
Gearbox	5-speed automatic
Installation	Front-engined / all-wheel drive
Front suspension	MacPherson strut
Rear suspension	Multi-link
Brakes front/rear	Discs / discs
Front tyres	215 / 45R17
Rear tyres	215 / 45R17
Length	4665 mm (183.7 in.)
Width	1730 mm (68.1 in.)
Height	1425 mm (56.1 in.)
Wheelbase	2670 mm (105.1 in.)
Track front/rear	1495 / 1490 mm (58.9 / 58.7 in.)
0–100 km/h (62 mph)	7.9 sec
Top speed	237 km/h (147 mph)
Fuel consumption	9.6 l / 100 km (29.4 mpg)
CO_2 emissions	229 g / km

The new Legacy and its Outback spin-off combine quite a strong road presence with a much more upmarket interior package. Subaru could still work on its exterior sportiness and visual solidity, though: after all, the Subaru name has lots of strength and performance attached to it in consumers' minds, after the company's well-deserved rally success. Soft, rounded forms make the cars appear just somehow too polite, rather than grasping the opportunity to capitalize on that motorsport heritage. The Outback is the more overtly off-road version of the Legacy, with the body raised a little to give additional suspension travel and wheel clearance. The specifications given in the table refer to the Legacy.

All models have a deep grille and projector headlamps, set low and so requiring small semicircular cutouts in the bumper. Flared wheel arches and a wide track create a stable, squat and muscular stance. The front wings have more curvature at their leading edge, while there are strong bonnet crease lines.

The facia, door trim, roof lining and grab-handles all benefit from new padded materials to bring Subaru in line with Europe's more prestigious marques. On turning the ignition key on the 3.0R version, the instruments light up and arc round to their maximum settings in an entertaining show of electro-luminescent muscle-flexing.

No Subaru would be complete without its symmetrical all-wheel-drive system. Each wheel has a sensor to detect slip and there are sensors to register front-to-rear G-force and side-to-side G-force, and steering wheel G-sensors to detect 'yaw-rate', the technical name for sudden swerves. The result of all this rapid data collection is for engine power to be reduced and braking applied to whatever wheel will best help the driver escape a collision, which can only be good.

Subaru R1e

The R1e is a fun little four-seater that echoes the design language used on the face of the B9 Scrambler. As in the case of the Scrambler, there is a passing reference to the past of Subaru's parent company, Fuji Heavy Industries, in the aircraft business. But in contrast, R1e is a funky, urban vehicle with a tight, compact shape and playful features, with an almost demonically happy 'visage' manifested in 'friendly' headlamps and a big 'grin' from the grille!

A rounded-off triangular profile can be seen not only in the front grilles, but also in the door mirrors, the body section running through the door to the rear lamps, and in the headlamps themselves.

Prominent wheel arches protrude to envelop the wheels in a sporty manner, and the rear corner tumbles inward towards the roof, confirming – at least visually – that here is a car that can be expected to have excellent roadholding despite its electric power unit that replaces a conventional petrol engine. The powerplant comprises a light, brushless motor and a high-energy manganese lithium-iron battery, which can be recharged via a single-phase 200V AC outlet like those used in the air-conditioning units of many Japanese homes. The problem with concept cars like this, though, is that you are never quite sure if all the packaging issues have been addressed; if it was put into production, for example, would it inevitably finish up longer as a result of its receiving a conventional petrol engine?

Subaru could do worse than put the R1e into production. It would make a small, affordable Subaru to encourage people to buy into this eclectic brand. It would also go some way towards redressing the imbalance of Subaru being known principally for its overtly sporty Impreza models.

Design	Andreas Zapatinas
Engine	Electric motor

Subaru R2

Design	Andreas Zapatinas
Engine	0.66 in-line 4
Power	47 kW (63 bhp) @ 6000 rpm
Torque	103 Nm (76 lb. ft.) @ 3200 rpm
Gearbox	7-speed manual
Installation	Front-engined / all-wheel drive

Subaru introduced the R2 minicar at the Tokyo Motor Show at the end of 2003. It's aimed solely at the Japanese market, and is the successor to the Pleo minicar. It is constructed on a completely new platform and weighs 70 kg (154 lb.) less than the Pleo; it also, for the first time, incorporates several components shared with cars made by General Motors, GM being a major Subaru stakeholder now.

In keeping with all the marque's concept cars launched at Tokyo, the R2 adopts the new Subaru front-end design meant to inspire a warm feeling for the aircraft heritage of Fuji Heavy Industries, Subaru's originator. Not that anyone's ever really heard of any of its planes, but never mind. On such a small car, the wing-inspired shape is not best exploited and appears over-fussy; the grille design is much more successful on the lower and much wider B9 Scrambler than on this tall, narrow city runabout. But for range consistency, Subaru has imposed its new grille on to the R2 anyway, and we can expect to see this identity systematically infiltrate all its other offerings.

The overall body is upright and rounded with the obvious emphasis on city practicality and good fuel economy. An interesting design feature along the side is the high positioning of the door rubbing strip, which extends into the side repeater lamps. It should ward off those inevitable urban parking knocks. For such a small car, the engine technology is advanced in a typically Subaru over-the-top way. Although only 660 cc, the engine has a supercharged four-cylinder twin overhead-camshaft configuration, with active valve control to provide a wide power range to the wheels through a seven-speed gearbox.

Suzuki Concept S2

Engine	1.6 in-line 4
Gearbox	6-speed manual
Installation	Front-engined / front-wheel drive
Length	3695 mm (145.6 in.)
Width	1730 mm (68.1 in.)
Height	1490 mm (58.7 in.)
Wheelbase	2390 mm (94.1 in.)

Suzuki's Concept S2 is a youthful, compact four-seater convertible that's an evolution of the Concept S launched in Paris in 2002. Suzuki claims it's looking to design compact cars that are fun to drive, and the S2 gives an idea for a new small car that, if we take the company at its word, will be manufactured from 2004.

A wrap-around glasshouse design hides the front pillars from view and shows the windscreen and windows at the front and sides as a single piece of glass – a critical part of the Concept S2's distinctive styling. The lurid pearl-yellow and white of early renderings was rather more garish than the bright red of the finished car, but the Concept S2 still exudes sporty, casual fun. The three-piece roof rotates and retracts, revealing seating space for four. When the roof is up, the interior colour is two-tone black and ivory. The roof lining has a playful 'blue sky' design motif, giving passengers a cartoonish feeling of Californian skies overhead even when the roof must be in place because it's bucketing down in Cologne.

The interior design combines a rounded basic form, harmonizing with the wrap-around window design outside and the instrument panel to project a solid impression. The Advanced Navigation System features an engaging (you could say distracting) on-screen female character serving as a virtual navigator. The system comes with various features, including a car-to-car mutual communication function so that you can share information on your road position, along with a display of real-time weather information for the area you're driving into – essential equipment, this, for an interactive convertible of the future!

Suzuki Landbreeze

Engine	0.66 in-line 3
Front suspension	3-link coil
Rear suspension	3-link coil
Front tyres	205 / 70R18
Rear tyres	205 / 70R18
Length	3500 mm (137.8 in.)
Width	1650 mm (65 in.)
Height	1680 mm (66.1 in.)
Wheelbase	2350 mm (92.5 in.)

The philosophy behind the Landbreeze concept is that here is a compact SUV that uses advanced environmental technologies so that it can, as Suzuki puts it with an embarrassing stab at poetic justi-fication, "co-exist with nature". Suzuki's idea is that a car should be designed to blend harmoniously with the land on which it drives. Why the company has chosen to demonstrate this on an SUV is, at the very least, a rather odd decision. There are much smaller vehicles possible – such as Suzuki's own, top-selling Wagon R+ microcar, which gnaws away at the world's natural resources comparatively sparingly – that have less environmental impact.

For a car supposed to project a comfortable synergy with the natural environment, the styling is very 'engineered'. Virtually no suggestion of organic design language is used anywhere. In fact, the boxy pro-portion is echoed throughout in design features: front grille, windows, lamps and underbody guards all use rounded-off cubic signatures. One good point, however, is the A-pillar, made larger so that a window can be fitted into it to improve visibility, much like Volvo's Safety Concept Car of two years ago.

Key environmental features of the Landbreeze include its lightweight aluminium body that can be fully recycled, along with resin body panels – although these are normally not possible to regurgitate to a virgin state, only becoming a reclaimed bulk 'filler' for other components. The tyres are made from non-petroleum resources, which is nice.

There is a dome-shaped monitor that sits on the dashboard and shows two different images, one to convey information to the driver and one for the passenger's benefit.

Overall, this is a concept of confused messages that seems, really, to represent ecological tokenism at its most patronizing.

Suzuki Mobile Terrace

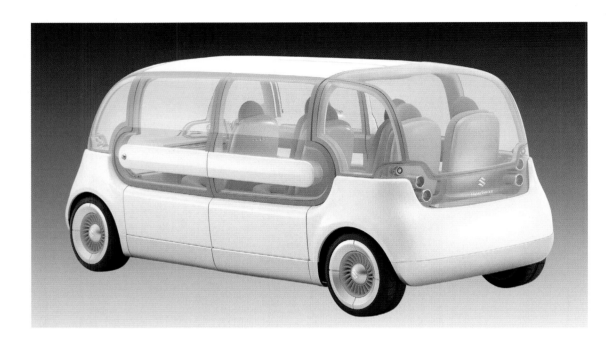

As the whacky name suggests, Mobile Terrace is an unconventional concept, and one that aims to allow as much light and air as possible into the 'car'. The name, in typically Japanese style, is disarmingly honest about its ambitions. It is a six-seater microbus powered by the same fuel-cell system used in General Motors' Hy-wire concept (GM has a large stake in Suzuki). Hence, it uses steer-by-wire and brake-by-wire technologies to free up space inside. This creates the possibility of three rows of seats in a vehicle 4 metres (13 ft.) long.

There are sliding doors on both sides and a gullwing-type roof to make the most of blue skies above; glass is used extensively for a feeling of freedom inside. The design of Mobile Terrace is unconventional to car design, almost like architecture with its choice of symmetrical forms and warm colour tones. It exudes tactility. The body eschews sharp edges: its overall form is rounded and so are the individual features.

Inside, the aim has been to create informal space. The seats rotate and slide outward, the instrument panel converts into an impromptu table and there is a large 22 in. monitor built into that instrument panel, controlled by a touch panel or by a speech-recognition system.

This car would certainly be magnificent to ride in, and would provide a truly unique motoring experience. Maybe it's the type of design that really will be possible once vehicle packaging is routinely based on Hy-wire-type technology. And that day cannot be far away.

Engine	200 single fuel cells generating 125–200 volts
Front suspension	Double wishbone
Rear suspension	Double wishbone
Front tyres	225/40R18
Rear tyres	225/40R18
Length	4050 mm (159.4 in.)
Width	1695 mm (66.7 in.)
Height	1740 mm (68.5 in.)
Wheelbase	3000 mm (118.1 in.)

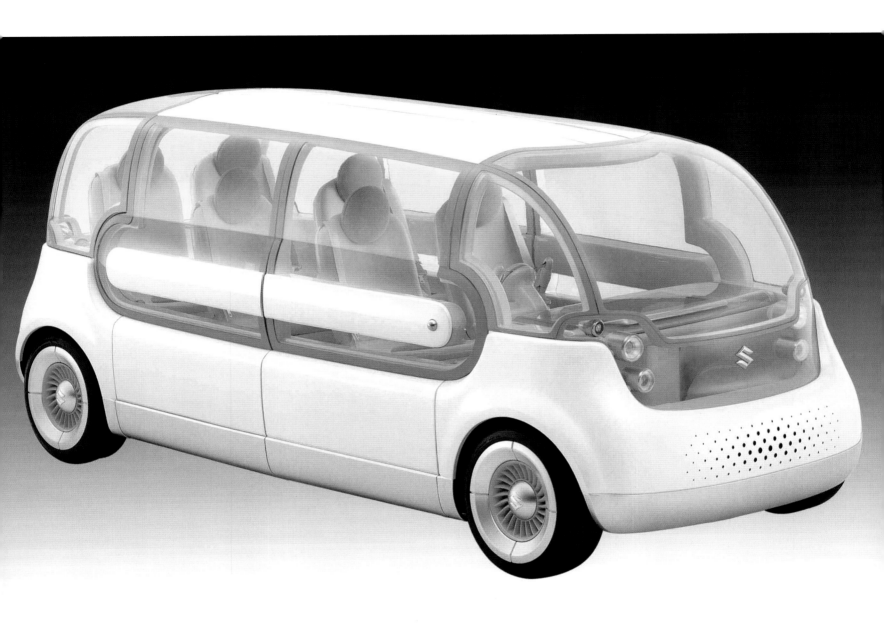

Suzuki S-Ride

Suzuki is one of those rare brands that manufactures both cars and motorcycles. BMW and Honda are the other protagonists, and Peugeot also does its own line in trendy scooters. With the S-Ride, both forms of transport are combined to create a new tandem two-seater car clearly targeting the young-driver market.

The S-Ride is, in essence, a small car built upon an aluminium spaceframe but without doors. Access is gained by opening the large canopy. It has the open-air feel of a motorcycle but with enough shelter from unforgiving elements to offer a car-like interior space. The telematics system has a function called 'lovers' sync', which allows the navigation system to guide the driver to the location of someone you are talking to on the phone. Pointless maybe, but you've got to admire the Japanese embrace of a cute idea at which their European counterparts would just scoff …

Its narrow body has wide tyres that project a picture of stability and presence. It is doubtful, however, that the driving experience would be anywhere near that of a motorcycle. As this four-wheeled 'car' is narrow, enthusiasm for cornering speeds would have to be moderated unless it was possible to build in some kind of automatic camber-countering system and fit special tyres. There is no evidence that Suzuki has considered this.

Diverting, certainly, but this is – sadly – a flawed concept. You would never get the true feeling of motor-cycle freedom and performance from it and, because of the tandem seating, you lose the sociable element of a car. S-Ride, at 1400 mm (55 in.) across, is slim but it is nowhere near narrow enough to benefit from the ability to weave through traffic like a motorcycle. BMW's C1 scooter had tandem seating and a roof, and could weave in and out of the traffic, yet it was a flop and has now been dropped. There is no real market for such a compromised car/motorcycle crossbreed: but celebrate the S-Ride simply for being an engaging showpiece nonetheless.

Engine	0.66 in-line 3
Gearbox	CVT
Front suspension	Double wishbone
Rear suspension	Double wishbone
Front tyres	175/50R17
Rear tyres	175/50R17
Length	3150 mm (124 in.)
Width	1400 mm (55.1 in.)
Height	1320 mm (52 in.)
Wheelbase	2160 mm (85 in.)

Toyota Corolla Verso

Engine	1.8 in-line 4 (1.6, and 2.0 diesel, also offered)
Power	96 kW (129 bhp) @ 6000 rpm
Torque	170 Nm (125 lb. ft.) @ 4200 rpm
Gearbox	5-speed manual
Installation	Front-engined / front-wheel drive
Front suspension	MacPherson strut
Rear suspension	Torsion beam
Brakes front/rear	Discs / discs
Front tyres	205 / 55R16
Rear tyres	205 / 55R16
Length	4360 mm (171.7 in.)
Width	1770 mm (69.7 in.)
Height	1620 mm (63.8 in.)
Wheelbase	2750 mm (108.7 in.)
Track front/rear	1505/1495 mm (59.3/58.9 in.)
Kerb weight	1355 kg (2987 lb.)
0–100 km/h (62 mph)	10.8 sec
Top speed	195 km/h (121 mph)
Fuel consumption	7.7 l/100 km (36.7 mpg)
CO_2 emissions	184 g/km

Ever wanted a practical, reliable and above all spacious car? Well, the new-generation Toyota Corolla Verso is all of that, but it is only available in Europe. With its seven seats and dynamic styling, added to Toyota's loyal and well-established customer base, this C-segment junior MPV is almost guaranteed to be a hit.

However, the Corolla Verso's exterior design was created at Toyota's European design studio, ED2, and the styling really struggles to project a unified message – it's not very 'together'. The huge headlamps seem out of proportion with the front-end design, especially with the grille, which looks dwarfed and irrelevant by comparison.

From the side, the body has well-defined, sporty wheel arches and protruding sills that lead the eye naturally to the wheels. The trouble is, these wheels are puny and very much at odds with the strong statement of the lower body's perimeter, as well as with the dynamic feel to the upper architecture characterized by the curved roof and triangular quarter-window.

All things considered, the Corolla Verso isn't the worst-looking car around, simply a quirky one, with its inverted L-shaped rear lamps. Maybe Toyota needs to focus on expressing pure functionality rather than trying to layer design features on top of a straightforward motoring box.

Inside, the dash is dark and geometric, with a metallic centre panel that helps to bring its somewhat humdrum surroundings to life. Yet it also has the effect of looking out of place as a consequence. Visually, it's too strong a feature for this family car – another example of trying too hard.

Toyota CS & S

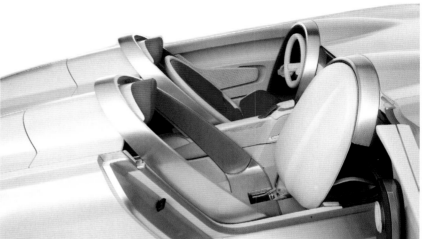

The CS&S from Toyota is one of those concepts you just can't take your eyes off. Requiring a double-take to check which is the front or the back, whether because of its unnerving symmetry or the missing windscreen, the CS&S is a real stunner. Its design clearly emphasizes the wheels and cockpit as focal points. 'Geometrical simplicity' accurately describes the overall structure, with large wheel arches and upper body bulges that all draw the eye.

An unusual technical concept is in the rear wheels. They're powered by a petrol engine, while the front ones are turned by an electric motor to complete a novel four-wheel-drive system. The combined benefits are high torque and economy from the electric motor, and increased driving range from the petrol one. No one seems to have considered this neat combination before but, then, Toyota was already a step ahead with its very successful Prius petrol-electric showroom model.

Toyota intends to develop this 'Hybrid Synergy Drive' philosophy further to introduce more powerful petrol and electric power sources that can hit higher levels of performance. Only a company of Toyota's technical research standing will be able to achieve such advances as this, spurred on by exacting Japanese environmental and congestion demands.

Inside, the front seats can rotate to cover completely the cockpit area. The seat design is shaped to reflect the curvy lines of the exterior, and arched shapes are repeated once again in the cockpit parameters. These define a clear environment for the driver and passenger, but also stress the car's innate sportiness. Another hi-tech feature is Toyota's Space Touch. This is an integrated multimedia system operated via a series of holographic projections that the user simply 'touches' to make a selection. Cool, huh?

Design	ED2 in France
Engine	1.5 in-line 4 (rear wheels) and electric motor (front wheels)
Installation	Mid-engined / four-wheel drive
Length	3940 mm (155.1 in.)
Width	1800 mm (70.8 in.)
Height	1120 mm (44.1 in.)
Wheelbase	2550 mm (100.4 in.)

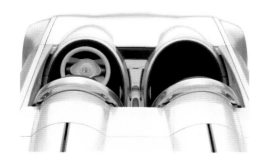

Toyota FTX

The FTX concept was designed at Toyota's research and design centre in Newport Beach, California. This full-sized pickup is designed to compete in the toughness stakes with Ford's F-150 and Nissan's Titan, and this is made very clear at the front with the huge, chrome grille surround that leads up to the high bonnet concealing the V8 powerplant.

Unusually for a truck, specific attention has been given to building surface form into the side of the body. Blistered wheel arches that 'waist in' at the cabin accentuate the massive wheels. Metallic-looking bumpers and sill covers add an element of resilience and also help to break up the massive pickup height.

This is a demanding vehicle with plenty of in-built functionality. Included in the bumpers are integrated tow hooks, and the rear skidplate houses an electric generator, an air compressor and other power outlets. Hidden away in the rear tailgate is an extendable ramp that reaches to the ground when the gate is open, allowing heavy items to be rolled up into the bed, instead of being lifted.

Inside, the design is one of angular architectural structures that embrace the occupants and mix together aluminium and earthy-coloured materials. A wide centre console separates at the 3D centre display screen and contains an armrest-mounted control-arm including all instrumentation and operational levers for the driver, who sits in a high and commanding position.

Every truck fanatic in America will have a natural soft spot for the FTX, while every car-mad kid will no doubt want a model of it.

Design	Craig Kember
Engine	V8 petrol-electric hybrid
Front tyres	355/55R22
Rear tyres	355/55R22
Length	5791 mm (228 in.)
Width	2095 mm (82.5 in.)
Height	1961 mm (77.2 in.)
Wheelbase	3805 mm (149.8 in.)

Toyota MTRC

Engine	Fuel-cell stack
Installation	In-wheel motors
Length	4060 mm (158.8 in.)
Width	1930 mm (76 in.)
Height	1330–1480 mm (52.4–58.3 in.)
Wheelbase	2950 mm (116.1 in.)

Designed and built by Toyota's European design studio, ED2, the Motor Triathlon Race Car (MTRC) is a fuel-cell-powered fantasy for many young kids today. This race car can be 'driven' by them too, as the MTRC features in Gran Turismo 4, the latest version of the enduringly popular Sony PlayStation game. It is designed to compete in a triathlon of different environments: an off-road course, a smooth and high-grip racetrack, and a narrow city-street circuit.

It is configured like a fighter-aircraft cockpit on wheels. The tandem seating arrangement allows for minimal frontal area and the suspension is all inboard and enclosed. It looks to be tremendous fun and the dramatic hinged cockpit roof looks fantastic when open. The driver and passenger wear special helmets that, like head-up displays, relay information on speed, upcoming roads and tyre condition to a screen inside them.

To help it compete on different surfaces, the car uses electronically controlled suspension that monitors road conditions and adjusts ride-height settings accordingly. 'Intelligent' tyres stiffen or soften to the prevailing road conditions through built-in sensors, matching grip to each surface. The wheels each have their own electric motor powered by the Toyota fuel-cell stack.

This is automotive escapism, pure and simple.

Toyota NLSV

The new NLSV concept from Toyota is a compact four-seater with a low floor and a high roof. This gives walk-in access and an especially user-friendly package. The interior is bright and cheerful, a warm lemon and grey combination to suit the young target customer. Because the body of the car is so tall, there is a large amount of glass above the waist rail that makes for excellent all-round visibility.

The front end is dominated by the huge bumper that juts forward from the grille, complete with black band and spotlamps, and headlamps that form a simple horizontal band across the vehicle to echo the simple form and lines throughout. The very short bonnet leads up on to a windscreen that creates a consistent arch over to the top of the boot lid.

At the side, a large electric-powered door slides backward to give excellent, unimpeded access. This is a very practical solution and one we should see more of on production cars in the years to come, if the slew of recent concepts are an accurate indicator. The fact that the door slides rather than opening away from the vehicle makes it possible to create bigger openings without the associated problems of big door 'swings' when parallel parking.

Length	3970 mm (156.3 in.)
Width	1690 mm (66.5 in.)
Height	1710 mm (67.3 in.)

Toyota PM

Here is a very exciting concept that really explores the idea of single-person transportation. It's just the sort of left-field design that has become a hallmark of the Tokyo Motor Show, which is likely to be the first and the last place you'll see it. And that's a shame.

To enter the PM, the driver must first touch one of its headlights that stick out on the end of stalks. This then glows green to signal the opening of the glass canopy. As the canopy opens, the driving seat slides down, forward and out so the driver can install himself or herself. Once behind the PM's controls, the car is easily manoeuvrable because the wheels turn through 180 degrees – thanks to being mounted on pivots like a caster. As the car gathers speed, it lowers and lengthens itself from 1750 mm (70 in.) to 2650 mm (104 in.) using rear hinges, which is aimed at making it more stable as it hugs the road closer. This is possible as the structures for the body and wheel suspension are separate. It is a similar idea to that used on the Renault Zoom concept car in 1992, although that incarnation of the 'folding' car was intended for ease of city parking.

The PM looks space-age thanks not only to its silvery, capsular appearance, but also to its futuristic wheels and tyres that appear to defy what is technologically possible today. The antenna-like headlamps are mounted at the base of the windscreen and look like they would change direction as needed, and give the appearance of an alien life form!

Inside, the driver cockpit, including the seat, is designed as a tightly fitting ergonomic space. A floating virtual display senses driver finger position and shows vehicle data, locations of other PMs on the road, and other such useful information. PM is an excellent concept that breaks with convention and explores selfish and fun motoring for one.

Engine	Electric motor
Length	1750–2650 mm (68.9–104.4 in.)
Width	1465 mm (57.7 in.)
Height	1215–1855 mm (47.8–73 in.)

Volkswagen Concept C

Engine	2.0 in-line 4
Power	112 kW (150 bhp)
Gearbox	6-speed manual
Brakes front/rear	Discs/discs
Front tyres	235/35ZR19
Rear tyres	245/35ZR20
Length	4410 mm (173.3 in.)
Width	1810 mm (71.3 in.)
Height	1430 mm (56.3 in.)

The Concept C is rather more than simply a styling exercise: now's the time to decide whether you like this new look, because it's sure to be the shape of things to come from Volkswagen.

The radiator grille has a new design that was first featured in the roadster design study the Concept R. It is made from aluminium and is combined with round headlights that are slightly shielded by the bonnet 'eyebrow'. The headlight, grille and front tapering swages have gone on to influence the bonnet too; it has a V-contour reproduced in a wide depression. The sides of the bonnet rise to create a curving look to the wing for a muscular appearance.

From the side, the silhouette shows a strong car with a large C-pillar but, at the rear, the boot tapers to emphasize cruising ability rather more than outright sportiness. The crease line running through the door emphasizes athleticism and gives a flair the rear end lacks.

As with most convertibles, the Concept C looks better with the roof down than up. This is not because it has some poorly designed canvas roof system; instead, it has a quickly folding metal roof with a built-in sunroof. When it's raised, the sportiness of the roof and cant rails do not complement the softer rear end, whereas when it's down the whole car is elegantly transformed.

Volkswagen Concept R

Design	Murat Günak
Engine	3.2 V6
Power	197 kW (265 bhp) @ 6250 rpm
Torque	350 Nm (258 lb. ft.) @ 2800 rpm
Gearbox	6-speed manual
Installation	Mid-engined / rear-wheel drive
Brakes front/rear	Discs / discs
Front tyres	255/40R19
Rear tyres	255/40R19
Length	4163 mm (163.9 in.)
Width	1778 mm (70 in.)
Height	1250 mm (49.2 in.)
Wheelbase	2580 mm (101.6 in.)
Track front/rear	1471/1491mm (57.9/58.7 in.)
0–100 km/h (62 mph)	5.3 sec
Top speed	250 km/h (155 mph) limited

At long last, a really sexy-looking sports car from Volkswagen. The new eye-like headlights here create a visage you would immediately associate with the Volkswagen brand, although the designers face a challenge to balance VW design lineage with the emotional, sporty language normally associated with this type of car. The bonnet continues the 'V' of the radiator grille and contours upward to the A-pillars. This V is then stressed by two flowing protrusions that separate the contoured wings from the gently curving bonnet. The wings appear more as independent structures.

As with the Phaeton, Touareg and new Golf, the Concept R's wing area is extended to the front above the headlights like an eyebrow. In line with the New Beetle, there are just three prominent lines that form the silhouette of the Concept R: two semicircles each for the high rise of the wheel arches and one straight line closing to a semicircle at the rear of the waistline.

Certain oblique references are made to sports cars of the 1950s, with such items as the petrol filler neck on the left of the bonnet finished in aluminium. Technology abounds, with keyless access to lock and unlock the doors, two body domes behind the driver and front passenger offering wind deflection and roll-over protection, and an integral GPS and GSM aerial.

Inside, you need sunglasses to ward off the dazzle from all that shiny chrome. One novel feature is that, as soon as the driver switches on the ignition to stand-by, the VW emblem begins to pulsate, stopping only when the ignition is activated.

Volkswagen Concept T

Engine	3.2 V6
Power	180 kW (241 bhp) @ 6250 rpm
Torque	320 Nm (236 lb. ft.) @ 2800 rpm
Installation	Front-engined / all-wheel drive
Front tyres	285 / 45R19
Rear tyres	285 / 45R19
Length	4079 mm (160.6 in.)
Width	1963 mm (77.3 in.)
Height	1450 mm (57.1 in.)
Wheelbase	2567 mm (101.1 in.)
Track front/rear	1620 / 1620 mm (63.8 / 63.8 in.)
0–100 km/h (62 mph)	6.9 sec
Top speed	232 km / h (144 mph)

Half sports car, half off-roader – this is Volkswagen's latest coupé concept car. In the United States especially, the market for SUVs is dominated by large off-roaders, and in this category you seldom find one that adds any sports car characteristics to the package. Also, there are no current production sports cars capable of driving off-road. VW claim to have filled this gap with the Concept T.

Stylistically, this search for a satisfying compromise results in a truly new shape. Viewed from the front, the Concept T echoes the Concept R roadster study. It shares the V-shaped radiator grille integrated into the bumper unit; variations of this will, according to insiders, distinguish the fronts of all new Volkswagens from now on.

The visually dramatic wing doors are mounted on the upper section of the A-pillars. When open, they simultaneously swing slightly outward and steeply upward, looking a bit like a ladybird in flight. The exterior mirrors are located high on the A-pillars to ensure visibility over the bulging rear wheel arches. To emphasize the Concept T's off-road character, lights front and rear appear to float in their bumper/wing housings by being set in matt-black surrounds; these contribute towards the effect of the whole upper body appearing simply to lie atop the hefty off-road chassis. Twin exhaust outlets are also well away from the ground for off-roading.

The trouble with a crossover of this type – and it's a theme that has been tackled time and again over the last twenty years – is its inevitable compromise. The car's centre of gravity is too high for excellent sports car handling, while the interior space is too compromised for a car with the SUV practicality vaunted by the vast majority of SUV choosers. The Concept T is, therefore, arresting but fundamentally flawed.

Volkswagen Golf

Design	Harmut Warkuss
Engine	2.0 in-line 4 (1.4 and 1.6, and 1.9 and 2.0 diesel, also offered)
Power	112 kW (150 bhp) @ 6000 rpm
Torque	200 Nm (147 lb. ft.) @ 3500 rpm
Gearbox	6-speed manual
Installation	Front-engined / front-wheel drive
Front suspension	MacPherson strut
Rear suspension	Multi-link
Brakes front/rear	Discs / discs
Front tyres	205 / 55R16
Rear tyres	205 / 55R16
Length	4204 mm (165.5 in.)
Width	1759 mm (69.3 in.)
Height	1485 mm (58.5 in.)
0–100 km/h (62 mph)	8.9 sec
Top speed	206 km/h (128 mph)
Fuel consumption	7.2 l/100 km (39.2 mpg)

Volkswagen's latest Golf has been revamped and is now a tiny bit sportier than the outgoing model. The front end now slopes more and the twin headlamps have a more piercing look, tapering towards the grille in the centre and giving a less linear feel to the face. The bonnet is lower in the middle over the grille and rises upward over the lamps to the top edge of the wing. These forms create a V-shaped effect at the front.

Apart from these, the diferences are relatively subtle. The new Golf's silhouette is defined by the rakish, wedge-shaped line below the side windows, the continuous side-window graphics, and the characteristic angle of the C-pillar and the elongated roof section that holds aloft the small roof spoiler. The substantial C-pillar is a traditional stylistic feature of the Golf; it imparts strength to the body by creating two parallel lines on the five-door version running, diagonally, forward from the upper C-pillar to the rear wheel arch.

At the rear, distinctive new tail lamps cut into the tailgate and feature twin round reflectors to echo the front lamp design. To open the boot lid, the prominent VW badge swings upward to reveal a recessed handle – great for keeping your hands free of road grime in bad weather.

There can be little doubt that, once again, Volkswagen is on to a winner with the new Golf. It's simply up to its marketing department to ensure that the trusted, rock-solid Golf remains as strong as ever in the mind of the consumer. Just as long as such rivals as the new Opel Astra fail to eclipse it, that should be simple enough.

Volvo S40 and V50

Design	Peter Horbury
Engine	2.4 in-line 5 (1.6 and 1.8 in-line 4, and 2.0 in-line 4 diesel, also offered)
Power	164 kW (220 bhp) @ 5000 rpm
Torque	320 Nm (236 lb. ft.) @ 1500–4800 rpm
Gearbox	6-speed manual
Installation	Front-engined / front-wheel drive
Front suspension	MacPherson strut
Rear suspension	Multi-link
Brakes front / rear	Discs / discs
Front tyres	215 / 45R18
Rear tyres	215 / 45R18
Length	4468 mm (175.9 in.)
Width	1770 mm (69.7 in.)
Height	1452 mm (57.2 in.)
Wheelbase	2640 mm (103.9 in.)
Track front / rear	1535 / 1531 mm (60.4 in.)
Kerb weight	1419 kg (3128 lb.)
0–100 km / h (62 mph)	6.8 sec
Top speed	240 km / h (150 mph)
Fuel consumption	8.7 l / 100 km (32.5 mpg)
CO$_2$ emissions	208 g / km

The exterior of the S40 saloon (shown opposite) is a carefully paced evolution of Volvo cars' modern body design. The grille, with its familiar diagonal bar, has a horizontal mesh pattern in a dark-grey metallic colour, similar to the Volvo S60 and S80. The bonnet has the traditional V-shape. The body's contour lines – the classic Volvo shoulders along either side of the body – are also inherited from the rest of the Volvo family. Those broad shoulders are a modern Volvo feature that signals power and safety, and they continue through to the distinctive tail lamps. The S40's doors are convex in profile, unlike the concave shape of the doors on the larger Volvo models. This convex curvature reinforces the compact appearance and enhances the width of the cabin. The specifications given in the table are for the S40.

The V50 estate version (shown above), meanwhile, has a roofline, complete with integral roof bars, that gradually reclines as the eye travels rearward towards the back of the car. Once there, the lamps dominate, drawing the eye outboard, visually widening the car and emphasizing those shoulders once again.

When it came to the interior, Volvo says it has used influences outside the automotive industry. There is a distinctly 'Scandinavian' aura to the clean surfaces and uncluttered lines, together with a pleasing lightness of materials and structures. True, every car-maker makes similar boasts, but Volvo quotes some specific sources of inspiration: Arne Jacobsen's classic compression-moulded Series 7 and Ant chairs, plus Alvar Aalto's typically Nordic functional architecture and furniture design.

Trends in hi-tech products such as audio systems, cameras and computers were a source of less specific inspiration, not just for form and function but also for ways of using and combining new materials. The result is the free-standing and 'floating' centre stack previewed recently in the Volvo VCC (Versatility Concept Car). There are a number of discreet lighting points, too, that give the effect of theatre lighting, with soft illumination of various parts of the interior.

Overall, a lot of careful effort has gone into giving these cars a character that such anodyne competitors as the Volkswagen Bora singularly lack.

Volvo YCC

Design	Anna Rosén
Engine	2.6 in-line 6
Power	186 kW (250 bhp)
Gearbox	Automated-shift manual
Installation	Front-engined/front-wheel drive
Brakes front/rear	Discs/discs
Length	4400 mm (173.2 in.)
Width	1830 mm (72 in.)
Height	1420–1480 mm (55.9–58.3 in.)
Wheelbase	2755 mm (108.5 in.)
Track front/rear	1595/1595 mm (62.8/62.8 in.)
Kerb weight	1300 kg (2866 lb.)
Fuel consumption	6.5 l/100 km (43.5 mpg)

In the United States, 54 per cent of all Volvo buyers are female, so there is real purpose to this novel project – a concept car designed exclusively by women. The YCC, for Your Concept Car, is tilted at the independent, professional woman, somebody Volvo claims is its most demanding and important customer. She wants performance, prestige and style, but also smart storage solutions, a car that is easy to get in and out of, good visibility, personalization opportunities, minimal maintenance and ease of parking.

The YCC exterior has been developed specifically to help the driver see better. The bonnet section is lowered and the wings deliberately brought into sight. The rear window extends right to the extremities of the car, so the driver should, theoretically, know the precise location of the four corners of the car. The gullwing-style doors are fantastic and very flamboyant, but would obviously be rather ambitious for a series production car.

The interior is the most radical part. The driver's heel-rest is fully adjustable because, of course, shoe heels can differ from one day to the next, while the head restraint has been adapted to cater for such hairstyles as ponytails. As you can imagine, tabloid newspapers have latched on to these details with gusto.

The gearlever is positioned near the steering wheel and the parking brake is electronic and integrated. This frees up space for storage in the centre console – the most easily accessible space in the car for the driver. Also within easy reach is a compartment for a notebook computer, a coolbox and a wastepaper basket. Instrumentation is simplified, with essentially only a speedometer, a distance indicator and a navigation system visible. There is also a parallel-parking assistance function that, first, checks that the space is big enough and, secondly, by selecting 'Autopark', controls the steering to help you manoeuvre into the space.

With so many excellent ideas – for men as well as women – it's easy to see why Volvo has made a big deal about this concept, and will use it as a spearhead for future marketing to affluent women customers. Will the YCC mark a serious shift in car design? It could but, first, more women need to graduate in automotive design, and that will only happen if there are exciting job opportunities ahead.

Profiles of Key Designers
Aerodynamics
Developments in Lighting

Wayne Cherry

Wayne Cherry retired as Vice-President of Design at General Motors on 1 January 2004, only the fifth holder of this critical role at GM. His career had spanned forty-two years at the company, during which he oversaw the renaissance of GM design.

Cherry was born in Indianapolis in 1938 and began his career in GM's Advanced Design Studio as an associate creative designer in 1962, after having graduated from the Los Angeles Art Center College of Design. His first major contribution was as part of the team that designed the incredible 1966 Oldsmobile Toronado and the first-generation Chevrolet Camaro in 1967, both of which rapidly became gold-plated classics.

Cherry spent much of the middle part of his career in Europe after moving to England in 1965, designing for GM's European subsidiaries Vauxhall and Opel. He became Director of Design for Vauxhall in 1971, overseeing the creation of such striking concept models as the Vauxhall SRV in 1970 and the Equus in 1978. For many years he was responsible for maintaining a distinctive identity for Vauxhall at a time (the mid-1970s) when its design activities were being wound down in anticipation of being centred on Opel in Germany, and he gave many future design stars, including Martin Smith and Ken Greenley, invaluable experience (and, no doubt, a zeal to advance their own careers beyond GM!) by recruiting them to work for Vauxhall's Bedford truck division. In addition, he oversaw a number of other concepts for Opel, in particular the Tech 1, from which the Opel Kadett/Vauxhall Astra of 1983 was derived.

Moving on to become Director of Design at Opel in Germany in 1983, Cherry now had overall responsibility for all of GM's now-united European design operations. In Germany his team backed up Opel's manufacturing and marketing success with a number of cars that included the Opel Junior concept – which heavily influenced the future Corsa – the Omega, the Calibra coupé and the Tigra. Cherry then returned to the United States, initially as executive designer for Chevrolet, Geo and GM of Canada. Then, in 1992, he got the top job, Vice-President of GM Design, taking over from the legendary Chuck Jordan.

By the late 1990s, Chrysler had ruled the American concept car scene for many years. In 1999 Cherry, with the support of industry guru and GM president Bob Lutz, launched an assault on the worldwide motor

Above
2003 Cadillac Sixteen

Opposite, clockwise from top
1970 Vauxhall SRV

1970 Vauxhall SRV

1981 Opel Tech 1

1981 Opel Tech 1, interior

show circuit that resulted in an incredible thirty-five concept cars being unveiled by the end of 2003 – more than any other manufacturer has managed over such a brief period. That's not far off one a month. Stimulating concepts included the Chevy SSR, and the Pontiac Solstice roadster and coupé, which created such a media stir that they were fast-tracked to the showroom.

Cherry has been a leading creative light in the blurring of traditional boundaries between conventional passenger sedans and the all-American truck that has resulted in the crossover car. The chiselled yet dynamic look of the Chevrolet Traverse concept of 2000, for example, showed that this real-life melding was a trend of the very near future.

In addition, in his position of latter-day design guru, he has spearheaded a recruitment drive for designers with innovative track records in the European sphere, boosting the car-design head-count at GM in Detroit; a notable coup for him was to recruit Anne Asensio from Renault, a key designer in the creation of the mould-breaking Renault Mégane Scenic.

In the latter years, Cherry had a pivotal role in creating the new identity, vision and design direction for Cadillac and Hummer that resulted in such bold production models as the Cadillac SRX and the Hummer H3, and such concepts as the amazing Cadillac Sixteen. GM's design direction has now been handed over to Ed Welburn, the sixth design chief in the company's ninety-five-year history. Thanks to Wayne Cherry, he has a firm base on which to build General Motors' extraordinarily wide design remit for the twenty-first century.

Opposite top
1978 Vauxhall Equus

Opposite bottom
1987 Opel Omega

Above
1992 Opel Calibra

Left
1983 Opel Junior Concept

Peter Horbury

Peter Douglas Horbury was born in Alnwick, Northumberland, on the north-east coast of England, in January 1950. His father taught him how to draw perspectives at the early age of four and by the age of eleven he had already decided that car design was the career he wanted. Much later, in 1972, he received a degree from the Newcastle-upon-Tyne College of Art and Industrial Design, following which, under sponsorship from Chrysler UK, he went on to complete a master's degree in automotive design at London's Royal College of Art in 1974.

Horbury's determination and commitment to his work across the globe is clear. He was named *Autocar* magazine's Designer of the Year in 1998 and, during his thirty-year career, he has been actively involved in the design of more than thirty-five cars, as well as trucks, buses and motorcycles.

Horbury began his career with Chrysler UK, recently formed from the American giant's merger of the British Rootes Group with Simca of France. The first model he worked on was the Simca Chrysler Horizon – which won the 1978 European Car of the Year award. After some years at Chrysler, he moved to Ford UK, where he worked on the best-selling Escort, Sierra and Granada models.

In 1979 Horbury joined Volvo as a design consultant, moving after two years to Volvo's studio in The Netherlands, where he worked mainly on the interiors of the cars in the Volvo 480 ES, 440 and 460 model family (the exterior work was the product of Britain's IAD consultancy). In 1986 he briefly returned to Britain, where he established the design department for another independent firm, MGA (Michael Gibbs Associates) Developments, an engineering consultancy with a wide-ranging variety of worldwide clients, among them Rolls-Royce.

It is in the last thirteen years, however, that Horbury has enjoyed his real success, and even fame. Since 1991 he has been Design Director of Volvo Car Corporation, overseeing studios in Sweden, Spain and California, and building strategy for Volvo's future design direction. This task began in earnest in 1992 with the Environmental Concept Car shown at the Paris Motor Show. This was a much-acclaimed design study hastily created to clothe a Volvo gas-turbine technology showcase, and would prove a stepping

Top
1987 Volvo 480 ES

Above
Peter Horbury

Right
1996 Volvo V40

stone in the genesis of the S80 saloon. Horbury has since been central in hauling Volvo into the twenty-first century, using a confidence-exuding roster that has ranged from the all-new XC90 in the market to the Volvo Safety Concept Car on the show circuit. He has managed cleverly to marry Volvo's renowned safety-conscious values with stylish new designs; these days, a Volvo purchase is not only a safe and practical one – it's a stylish one too. Volvo's worthy but increasingly dull boxiness has been ditched. Long-standing customers don't seem to have minded too much, while fresh ones have found the new direction enticing. Now, as part of the bigger Ford empire, Volvo plays a significant role, especially in the highly sensitive area of vehicle safety.

In 2002 Peter Horbury moved to the exalted position of Executive Director of Design for Ford's Premier Automotive Group, giving him responsibility for overseeing product-design strategy for Aston Martin, Jaguar, Land Rover and Volvo. Few car designers have ever been steward to such a diverse and influential design legacy as these marques possess between them.

Owing to Ford's recent upheavals in the United States, the company repositioned Horbury as Executive Director of Design, North America, in January 2004. This new role means that he is responsible for overseeing design strategy and execution for all Ford, Lincoln and Mercury products in North America. His freedom to shape the look of all the original marques of the 'mother ship' shows how much faith Ford's board has in his ability. Yet reversing the fortunes of these venerable but troubled brands will be his toughest test.

Opposite top
1985 Ford Sierra RS Cosworth

Opposite bottom
1978 Simca Chrysler Horizon

Above
2002 Volvo XC-90

Right
1992 Volvo ECC

Andrea Zagato

Andrea Zagato was born in Milan on 26 April 1960. He graduated from Milan's Bocconi University with a degree in economics and commerce, writing his dissertation on 'Design in the production and marketing of automobiles'.

This was hardly a surprising choice of subject-matter, because he is the son of Elio Zagato and the grandson of Ugo Zagato, who founded the legendary Zagato coachworks in 1919. Where Ugo broke new ground and set his company apart from rivals was in the way he embraced aeronautical construction techniques in the expanding market for lightweight sports cars.

Zagato's cars quickly became synonymous with low weight, pleasingly simple styling and excellent aerodynamics, making them eminently suitable for use as racing cars. Alfa Romeo, Fiat and Lancia immediately recognized the advantages of Zagato's rakish, streamlined output, and many collaborations followed, from – typically – the Alfa Romeo 1750SS of the vintage period (1918–31) to the Alfa Romeo SZ of the early 1990s. The most acclaimed creation is probably the Zagato-bodied Aston Martin DB4GTZ (1960), although the Zagato *carrozzeria*'s often idiosyncratic 1960s designs from the drawing board of its great in-house stylist Ercole Spada have ranged from Hillman Imps to Osca 1600s, and from Rover 2000s to Lamborghini 350GTs.

After graduating, the obvious step for Andrea was to join the august family firm. He initially worked in the field of communications, then in finance and control, and finally in contract management. The first design that he could call his own was a novel concept based on the Fiat Cinquecento, the 1992 Z-Eco, which put the two passengers in tandem on one side of the car, and an electric bicycle complete with recharging equipment on the other, as the perfect combination for suburban and city personal transport. The first project he had complete responsibility for, however, was the delightful Hyena coupé, based on the Lancia Delta Integrale, of which a small number were built in 1993.

The company went through a financial crisis that year, since which time its traditional coachbuilding activities have ceased. The design side, however, has grown quickly. Andrea and his wife Marella now run

Above
Andrea Zagato with, from left to right, a 1991 Alfa Romeo RZ, a 1952 Fiat 8V and a one-off 1968 Lancia Fulvia Spider, all with Zagato coachwork

Opposite
1992 Fiat 500 Z-Eco

the business together and have revived the image of the family firm, turning the historic Zagato premises at Terrazzano di Rho, outside Milan, into a bustling design bureau very much in the manner of Italdesign or IDEA. The main design and engineering offices, together with a museum of Zagato cars, are located in Milan, but the company also has a satellite studio in Florida, which is connected through a computer network, allowing designers and engineers on two continents to work together on automotive, marine and industrial-design projects.

A seventy-strong Italian workforce styles, builds and engineers prototypes, concept cars and show-stoppers. Although it was not actually an original Zagato design, the company created Fiat's Ecobasic of 2000, a major influence on its European Car of the Year in 2004, the new Panda. Frustratingly, the Andrea Zagato-penned L147 Lamborghini supercar was on the verge of entering production when Audi bought Lamborghini and cancelled the project in favour of the Murciélago in 1999. More happily, however, the company has once again struck up a relationship with Aston Martin, creating a distinctively different DB7Z limited-edition model in both coupé and roadster forms.

Over a period of eighty-five years, the Zagato name has been seen on designs, prototypes and concept cars for major car-makers in Italy, England, the United States, Germany, Japan and Sweden. Indeed, Zagato has created more than 200 cars in its illustrious, family-controlled history, and Andrea Zagato is known throughout the industry for taking this heavy responsibility very seriously. Yet he is not afraid to branch out, one interesting example being his company's design for Milan's sleek new Eurotram. Its aim of setting out to envision 'a very high-performing vehicle which … provides users of urban transport with maximum comfort and elegance' was so impressive that it scooped the 2002 Compasso d'Oro, Italy's most coveted industrial-design trophy.

Top
2002 Aston Martin DB7 Zagato

Above
2001 Lamborghini L147

Opposite from top
1998 Zagato Zuma
1996 Zagato Raptor

Aerodynamics

Whether designing the world's fastest car or the world's most economical, the planned management of airflow over a moving car's surface is absolutely critical to its performance. This is the essence of automotive aerodynamics.

The design elements of some cars are largely dominated by engineering principles. This is certainly the case for aerodynamic shapes, whether a car is designed to be either very fast or very fuel-efficient. This need for 'slippery' shapes means that aerodynamics has played a significant role in the evolution of car design, and this has, in turn, driven advances in manufacturing technologies for such items as headlamps, which can now be moulded into complex, wind-cheating forms.

Designing for aerodynamics is complex and all-encompassing. It affects so many aspects: the way a car looks, its fuel efficiency, how fast it goes, how noisy it is for the occupants, how stable it is on the road. It also has implications for the performance of such major areas as engine cooling, air-conditioning, brake performance and engine air induction. So many systems are affected by the aerodynamic control of airflow that, done properly, it can contribute significantly to overall perception of a car's quality.

The lower the 'coefficient of drag' – the answer to a complex equation calculated from data gathered by an aerodynamicist, and usually referred to as the 'Cd figure' or 'Cd factor' – the more slippery the car. Twenty years ago, a typical new American saloon car had a Cd of 0.48; today, that figure has been hugely reduced, to 0.33, and the very best mass-produced cars often achieve 0.28. Pickup trucks and SUVs, with their 'choppy' shapes that often ride higher up from road level, usually have Cds that are more than 0.44. Manufacturers are developing cars that will approach and, eventually, surpass the aerodynamic holy grail of Cd 0.2.

Reducing the Cd involves having a wedge-shaped front-end design with a small frontal area that can cut cleanly through the air. The rear of the car is equally critical: if turbulence created here (as airflow is left behind) can be minimized, then this has a big effect in reducing drag.

Look at the world's fastest cars, such as the 371 km/h (231 mph) McLaren F1, and you will notice that

Above
The world's fastest cars, such as the McLaren F1, are designed primarily for low drag and high downforce.

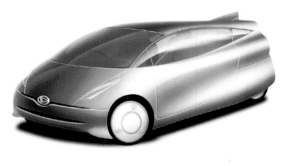

the cross-sectional area of the car viewed from the front is very low, to minimize the amount of air that needs to be displaced as the car travels along. This results in a very low car with a cockpit that fits snugly around the occupants.

However, at speeds of 300 km/h (190 mph), high-performance sports cars, such as Ferraris, encounter the problem of aerodynamic forces that tend to lift them into the air. This is caused by the upper surface of the body acting like a wing, speeding up the air and offering less resistance to it. To generate a downward force to keep the car stable and ensure good high-speed roadholding, spoilers or airdams are often used. But for aesthetic reasons, car designers are keen to avoid spoilers: designing the external shape of a car to achieve aerodynamic behaviour that pushes the car towards the ground while also satisfying aesthetic demands is a considerable challenge. 'Active' aerodynamics can be the answer.

When cornering at speed, downforce needs to be higher to increase the grip, whereas at lower speeds the extra drag and unsightly look of spoilers may be undesirable. A typical active aerodynamic feature is a rear spoiler that raises only when the car reaches a speed where it is needed – usually around 80 km/h (50 mph).

To generate high downforce for enhanced high-speed stability and cornering capability, such cars as the Ferrari 360 Modena use the underbody. The 360 Modena has a flat underbody with large rear air extractors: as speed increases, so does downforce, and the car's ground clearance is reduced as the air is sucked out from underneath it. The process eventually stops when equilibrium exists between the aerodynamic downforce and the elastic reaction of the suspension's springs.

Many of the technical brains behind today's higher-end luxury cars have paid close attention to the aerodynamics of the underside of the car, creating a smooth surface that gently slopes up towards the tail. Not only does this treatment decrease drag, it also reduces dangerous lift forces that can make a car unstable at high speed.

Techniques for simulating aerodynamic flow have been used for several years. Computational fluid dynamics (CFD) offers a mathematical approach to assessing how air will flow over an object. This is then

Top
Such cars as the Ferrari 360 Modena not only manage the airflow over the car so as to minimize drag but also use the flow under the car to generate downforce.

Above
The Daihatsu UFE-II concept displays the body proportion, and in particular the waisted rear, necessary to achieve a very low drag coefficient.

correlated with physical testing of scale models in a wind tunnel. It can target areas of the body needing change to improve airflow right at the very outset of a vehicle project, working alongside the styling programme and well before prototypes are made. CFD analysis has been used for spacecraft and aircraft design, and has now been adopted with some success in car design. It can reliably predict airflow and drag over a complete car shape rather than looking at the effects of much more complex problems, such as noise created by turbulent flow around a door seal, or large volumes of unsteady airflow, a typical example being the crosswind stability effect of overtaking lorries on a motorway. The main CFD limitation is that the analysis models are hugely complex.

Much more attention is also paid today to the reduction of 'aerodynamic noise', something that has come to the fore since engine and road noise have been so significantly reduced and suppressed. Aerodynamic noise is created by turbulent wind flow against the car body, often in such areas as the door windows where the flow is interrupted slightly around the windscreen and A-pillars. By designing the upper body of a car so as to control the airflow past the windows in as laminar (streamlined) a way as possible, turbulence, vortices and, hence, noise are reduced. Window seal design plays a vital part here, allowing the glass to sit as flush as possible to the rest of the body. This ensures minimal disturbance of air as it crosses the body, seals and side glass.

At the opposite end of the aerodynamic spectrum are cars that are not designed to go fast at all, but are designed to conserve fuel. These cars are usually light in weight and slippery in shape, and are typified by the Daihatsu UFE-II. The major drawback with this approach is that such cars are particularly sensitive to crosswinds. Nevertheless, emissions legislation in the future will undoubtedly drive manufacturers towards ever lighter vehicles, and reduced mass will exaggerate the effects of aerodynamic forces. Aerodynamic lateral thinkers, please step this way ...

Aerodynamic drag puts the greatest demand on a car's engine at highway speeds, even on level ground. Careful aerodynamic design can reduce the horsepower and, thus, the fuel needed to push a car

Top
Wind tunnel testing plays an important role in the development of fast cars right from the concept design. Advanced wind tunnels such as this one testing the Mercedes-Benz SLR have rollers that allow the wheels to revolve, creating a more realistic situation.

Above
Early wind tunnel testing involved the use of pieces of tape stuck to the car body, as seen here on the Volkswagen Beetle. The behaviour of the tape demonstrated whether the flow was laminar or whether there was turbulence-induced drag.

along at 110 km/h (70 mph). By combining careful aerodynamic design with hybrid-electric drive-trains, it is possible to create very efficient cars. The Honda Insight, for example, achieves 4 litres per 100 km (70 mpg) fuel efficiency on the highway.

Doubling a car's speed means that the engine must put out eight times more power to overcome air resistance, so even small reductions in drag can greatly reduce the power, size and cost of the engine needed to push the car along. Even though the body of most modern cars is smoother than the underbelly, a car's body can often be improved. Every protrusion creates drag, so designers must be mindful to minimize seams between body panels, hide windscreen wipers and even, maybe, replace side mirrors with flush-mounted miniature video cameras – this would also eliminate blind spots. Slightly tapering the entire body shape towards the tail can reduce drag forces.

We have shown that designing a vehicle with excellent aerodynamics can benefit the user in several ways, principally through greater speed, reduced fuel consumption and better noise refinement. The necessity for designing aerodynamic vehicles that conserve fuel will become more urgent as fuel prices escalate, making low-drag vehicles more attractive to those who want cheaper motoring. This option is already available to people, although with the number of SUVs and high-performance cars that are bought worldwide, you wouldn't believe it; perhaps the advances in engine technology that give better efficiency have negated the effect; or perhaps fuel is still too affordable.

Top
Designing for practicality together with high fuel economy is a real challenge for car-makers. The Honda Insight shows that it can be done – but at the price of style.

Above
The macho Hummer H2 ignores aerodynamic design altogether, since it is less important for a slow-moving and heavy vehicle.

Developments in Lighting

Right from the time when the very first candle and paraffin lamps were fitted to pioneering motor cars in the late nineteenth century, headlamps have played a huge part in shaping the 'face' of the car. As technology has advanced, so lighting has become much brighter, improving safety for drivers and other road users. Importantly, ever since America's Pierce Arrow became the first car-maker to integrate headlamps into the front mudguards in 1913, designers have been able to adapt headlamps into their overall work. Advances in manufacturing technology have also meant that pretty much any shape of lamp is now feasible.

Indeed, technical advances have driven headlamp design for more than eighty years, ever since the introduction of the twin-filament bulb in 1924 enabled a headlamp to produce both a symmetrical dipped beam and a main beam. Industry techniques limited the headlamp's shape to being circular until 1961, when the first rectangular headlamps were used on the Ford Taunus 17M, a ground-breaking family saloon designed by Uwe Bahnsen, who would later create the Ford Sierra. By the early 1950s, however, glass had given way in rear lamp lenses to thermoplastics, which allowed designers much greater freedom to mould the shape of the lamps to follow the bodywork's contours; rear fog lamps were added from 1966.

German light-maker Hella was the first to perfect halogen bulbs, which made their debut in the 1971-model Volkswagen Beetle. The vastly superior illumination they gave meant that they fast became the industry standard, and they remain commonplace to this day. Saab added an extra dimension by introducing a wash/wiper system for headlights on the 99 that same year.

During the 1980s designers began wondering why they couldn't have smaller headlamps to allow them to achieve better vehicle aerodynamics. Retractable, rotating headlights had been tried by Cord in the 1930s, but pop-up headlights – as fitted to models as diverse as the 1968 Chevrolet Corvette, the 1975 Triumph TR7 and Lotus Elite, and the 1983 Honda Prelude – appeared to ignore the fact that aerodynamics was just as important after dark, and that two drag-inducing upright boxes didn't help it.

In answer to this growing demand, in 1986 the DE (for *Dreiachsiger Elliptischer*) reflector headlamp made its first appearance on the BMW 7 Series. The DE comprises a halogen bulb, an ellipsoid reflector, a

Above left
1961 Ford Taunus 17M: the first rectangular headlamp

Above
1971 Volkswagen Beetle: the first use of the halogen bulb

Opposite top
1980 Triumph TR7, with pop-up lamps to improve aerodynamics (when the lamps are in their lowered position, flush with the body)

Opposite bottom
1986 BMW 7 Series: the first use of the DE reflector headlamp

shield and a lens. It is based on a triaxial elliptical reflector that doubles the amount of light output compared with traditional parabolic reflectors. Using this system, headlamps could be much reduced in size but offer undiminished light output.

As digital technology began to play an increasingly prominent role in overall car design, complex computer calculations resulted in the development of FF (free form) reflectors, producing light dispersal that obviated the need for optical patterning in the cover lens itself. The practical result of this was that it was possible to increase light output by 43 per cent more than a DE headlamp, giving designers even greater freedom to produce cars with even smaller lamps, together with a see-through surface style that, once again, has now become commonplace.

Another recent development is the xenon headlamp. A xenon 'bulb' does not have a coiled filament, but instead generates light from an electric arc. Inside the bulb, xenon gas is mixed with metallic salts and ignited by 20,000 volts, thus creating a piercing light source. Xenon headlamps first went into volume production with BMW.

Also in the early 1990s, headlamps with plastic lenses reduced weight (by up to 1 kg, just over 2 lb., per unit) and increased design freedom further, although this was made possible not by designer pressure but by changes in EU regulations.

So what of the future? Top-spec Mercedes-Benz models already feature 'bend-system' lighting, which angles the light into a bend when cornering. Such systems look set to become increasingly widespread, as will higher-powered xenon lamps. Yet the future of car lamp design probably lies squarely with light-emitting diodes, or LEDs. Recent LED advances have for the first time made them bright enough to be incorporated into headlights. This technology is making it possible to produce innovative new headlight designs that not only capitalize on the compact size of LEDs but also consume less energy than standard lamps and do not need to be replaced for the life of the car. The US-spec BMW 3 Series convertible, incidentally, was the first series-produced vehicle to have an LED safety brake light, back in 1992.

This page from top
2000 Alfa Romeo Spider: an example of FF (free form) technology

2004 Range Rover: an example of a clear plastic lens

Opposite from top
2004 Mercedes-Benz CLS, showing bend-system xenon lighting, which responds to the steering wheel angle by pointing the headlamp beam into the turn

2004 Fioravanti Kite concept: an example of LED technology

Technical Glossary
Where the New Models were Launched
Major International Motor Shows 2004–2005
Marques and their Parent Companies

Technical Glossary

Specification tables

The following list explains the terminology used in the specification tables that accompany the model descriptions. The amount of data available for any given model depends on its status as a concept or a production car. More information is usually available for models currently in or nearing production.

Engine	Engine size is quoted in litres, and refers to the swept volume of the cylinders per crankshaft rotation; 6.0, for example, means a 6 litre (or 6000 cc) engine. 'In-line' or 'V' followed by a number refers to the engine's number of cylinders. An in-line 4 engine has four cylinders in a single row, while a V8 engine has eight cylinders arranged in a V-formation. In-line engines of more than six cylinders are rare today because they take up too much packaging space – an in-line 12, for instance, would require a very long bonnet. Only Volkswagen makes a W12, an engine with its twelve cylinders arranged in a W-formation. The configuration of cylinders is usually chosen on cost grounds: the higher the car's retail price, the more cylinders product planners can include.
Power	Engine power is given in both metric kilowatts (kW) and imperial brake horsepower (bhp). Both are calculated at optimum engine crankshaft speed, given in revolutions per minute (rpm) by manufacturers as a 'net' measurement – in other words, an engine's output after power has been sapped by other equipment and the exhaust system – and measured by a 'brake' applied to the driveshaft.
Torque	Simply the motion of twisting or turning, in car terms torque means pulling power, generated by twisting force from the engine crankshaft. It is given in newton metres (Nm) and pounds feet (lb. ft.). The higher the torque, the more force the engine can apply to the driven wheels.
Gearbox	The mechanical means by which power is transmitted from the engine to the driven wheels. There is a wide variety of manual (with a clutch) and automatic (clutchless) versions. There have been recent trends for clutchless manual systems, called 'semi-automatic' or 'automated manual', and automatics with an option to change gear manually, sometimes called 'Tiptronic', 'Steptronic' or 'Easytronic'. 'CVT' (continuously variable transmission) refers to an automatic with a single 'speed': the system uses rubber or steel belts to take engine power to the driven wheels, with drive pulleys that expand and contract to vary the gearing. A 'sequential manual' is a manual gearbox with preset gear ratios that are ordered sequentially.
Suspension	All suspension systems cushion the car against road or terrain conditions to maximize comfort, safety and road holding. Heavy and off-road vehicles use 'rigid axles' at the rear or front and rear; these are suspended using robust, leaf-type springs and steel 'wishbones' with 'trailing arms'. 'Semi-rigid axles' are often found at the back on front-wheel-drive cars, in conjunction with a 'torsion-beam' trailing-arm axle. 'Independent' suspension means each wheel can move up and down on its own, often with the help of 'trailing arms' or 'semi-trailing arms'. A 'MacPherson strut', named after its inventor, a Ford engineer called Earl MacPherson, is a suspension upright, fixed to the car's structure above the top of the tyre. It carries the wheel hub at the bottom and incorporates a hydraulic damper. It activates a coil spring and, when fitted at the front, turns with the wheel.

Brakes	Almost all modern cars feature disc brakes all round. A few low-powered models still feature drum brakes at the back for cost reasons. 'ABS' (anti-lock braking system) is increasingly fitted to all cars: it regulates brake application to prevent the brakes locking in an emergency or slippery conditions. 'BA' (brake assist) is a system that does this electro-hydraulically, while 'EBD' (electronic brake-force distribution) is a pressure regulator that, in braking, spreads the car's weight more evenly so that the brakes do not lock. 'ESP' (electronic stability programme) is Mercedes-Benz's electronically controlled system that helps keep the car pointing in the right direction at high speeds; sensors detect wayward road holding and apply the brakes indirectly to correct it. 'Dynamic stability' is a similar system. 'Brake-by-wire' is a totally electronic braking system that sends signals from brake pedal to brakes with no mechanical actuation whatsoever. 'TCS' (traction-control system) is a feature that holds acceleration slip within acceptable levels to prevent wheelspin and therefore improves adhesion to the road. 'VSC' (vehicle stability control) is the computer-controlled application of anti-lock braking to all four wheels individually to prevent dangerous skidding during cornering.
Tyres	The size and type of wheels and tyres are given in the internationally accepted formula. Representative examples include: 315/70R17, 235/50VR18, 225/50WR17, 235/40Z18 and 225/40ZR18. In all cases the number before the slash is the tyre width in millimetres. The number after the slash is the height-to-width ratio of the tyre section as a percentage. The letter R denotes radial construction. Letters preceding R are a guide to the tyre's speed rating, denoting the maximum safe operating speed. H tyres can be used at speeds up to 210 km/h (130 mph), V up to 240 km/h (150 mph), W up to 270 km/h (170 mph) and Y up to 300 km/h (190 mph). Finally, the last number is the diameter of the wheel in inches. A 'PAX' is a wheel-and-tyre in one unit, developed by Michelin (for example, 19/245 PAX means a 19 in. wheel with a 245 mm tyre width). The rubber tyre element is clipped to the steel wheel part, rather than held on by pressure. The height of the tyre walls is reduced, which can free up space for better internal packaging, or for bigger wheels for concept car looks. It can also run flat for 200 km at 80 km/h, eliminating the need for a spare.
Wheelbase	The exact distance between the centre of the front wheel and centre of the rear wheel.
Track front/rear	The exact distance between the centre of the front or rear tyres, measured across the car at the ground.
Kerb weight	The amount a car weighs with a tank of fuel, all oils and coolants topped up, and all standard equipment but no occupants.
CO_2 emissions	Carbon dioxide emissions, which are a direct result of fuel consumption. CO_2 contributes to the atmospheric 'greenhouse effect'. Less than 100 g/km is a very low emission, 150 g/km is good, 300 g/km is bad. 'PZEV' (partial zero emission vehicle) refers to a low-level emission standard that was created to allow flexibility on ZEV standards in California.

Other terms

A-, B-, C-, D-pillars	Vertical roof-support posts that form part of a car's bodywork. The A-pillar sits between windscreen and front door, the B-pillar between front and rear doors, the C-pillar between rear doors and rear window, hatchback or estate rear-side windows, and the D-pillar (on an estate) between rear side windows and tailgate. Confusingly, however, some designs refer to the central pillar between front and rear doors as a B-pillar where it faces the front door and a C-pillar where it faces the rear one.

All-wheel drive	A system delivering the appropriate amount of engine torque to each wheel via a propshaft and differentials, to ensure that tyre slippage on the road surface is individually controlled. This system is ideal for high-performance road cars, such as Audis, where it's called 'quattro'.
Cant rail	The structural beam that runs along the tops of the doors.
Coefficient of drag	Also known as the Cd, this is shorthand for the complex scientific equation that proves how aerodynamic a car is. The Citroën C-Airdream, for example, has a Cd of 0.28, but the Citroën SM of thirty years ago measured just 0.24, so little has changed in this respect. 'Drag' means the resistance of a body to airflow, and low drag means better penetration, less friction and therefore more efficiency, although sometimes poor dynamic stability.
Diffuser	This is a custom-designed airflow conduit, often incorporated under the rear floor on high-performance and competition cars, which controls and evenly distributes fast-moving airflow out from beneath the speeding car. This ducting arrangement slows the flow of rushing air behind the car, lowering its pressure and so increasing aerodynamic downforce. The result is improved road-holding.
Drive-by-wire technology	Increasingly featured on new cars, these systems do away with mechanical elements and replace them by wires transmitting electronic signals to activate such functions as brakes and steering.
Drivetrain	The assembly of 'organs' that gives a car motive power: engine, gearbox, driveshaft, wheels, brakes, suspension and steering. This grouping is also loosely known these days as a 'chassis', and can be transplanted into several different models to save on development costs.
Fastback	This refers to the profile of a hatchback that has a rear screen at a shallow angle, so that the tailgate forms a constant surface from the rear of the roof to the very tail end of the car.
Feature line	A styling detail usually added to a design to differentiate it from its rivals, and generally not related to such functional areas as door apertures.
Four-wheel drive	This refers to a system delivering a car's power to its four wheels. In a typical 'off-road'-type four-wheel-drive vehicle, the differentials can be locked so that all four wheels move in a forward direction even if the tyres are losing grip with the road surface. This makes four-wheel drive useful when travelling across uneven terrain.
Greenhouse	The car-design industry's informal term for the glazed area of the passenger compartment that usually sits above the car's waist level.
Instrument panel	The trim panel that sits in front of the driver and front passenger.
Monospace/ monovolume/'one-box'	A 'box' is one of the major volumetric components of a car's architecture. In a traditional saloon, there are three boxes: one for the engine, one for the passengers and one for the luggage. A hatchback, missing a boot, is a 'two-box' car, while a large MPV such as the Renault Espace is a 'one-box' design, also known as a 'monospace' or 'monovolume'.
MPV	Short for 'multi-purpose vehicle', this term is applied to tall, spacious cars that can carry at least five passengers, and often as many as nine, or versatile combinations of people and cargo. The 1983 Chrysler Voyager and 1984 Renault Espace were the first. The 1977 Matra Rancho was the very first 'mini-MPV', but the 1991 Mitsubishi Space Runner was the first in the modern idiom.
Packaging space	Any three-dimensional zone in a vehicle that is occupied by component parts or used during operation of the vehicle.

Platform	Also known as the 'floorpan': the invisible, but elemental and expensive, basic structure of a modern car. It is the task of contemporary car designers to achieve maximum aesthetic diversity from a single platform.
Powertrain	The engine, gearbox and transmission 'package' of a car.
Spaceframe	A structural frame that supports a car's mechanical systems and cosmetic panels.
Splitter	Sometimes found at the front of high-performance cars near to ground level, this is a system of under-car ducting that splits the airflow sucked under the car as it moves forward, so the appropriate volume of cooling air is distributed to both radiator and brakes.
Sub-compact	You need to rewind fifty-four years for the origins: in 1950, Nash launched its Rambler, a two-door model smaller than other mainstream American sedans. The company coined the term 'compact' for it although, by European standards, it was still a large car. Nash's descendant American Motors then invented the 'sub-compact' class in 1970 with the AMC Gremlin, a model with a conventional bonnet and a sharply truncated hatchback tail; this was quickly followed by the similar Ford Pinto and Chevrolet Vega. In the international car industry today, 'sub-compact' is used as another term for 'A-segment', the smallest range of cars, intended mostly for city driving.
SUV	Short for 'sports utility vehicle', a four-wheel-drive car designed for leisure off-road driving but not necessarily agricultural or industrial use. Therefore a Land Rover Defender is not an SUV, while a Land Rover Freelander is. The line between the two is sometimes difficult to draw, and identifying a pioneer is tricky: SUVs as we know them today were defined by Jeep in 1986 with the Wrangler, Suzuki in 1988 with the Vitara, and Daihatsu in 1989 with the Sportrak.
Swage line	A groove or moulding employed on a flat surface to stiffen it against warping or vibration. In cars, swage lines add 'creases' to bodywork surfaces, enabling designers to bring visual, essentially two-dimensional interest to body panels that might otherwise look slab-sided or barrel-like.
Targa	Porsche had been very successful in the Targa Florio road races in Sicily, so, in celebration, in 1965 the company applied the name 'Targa' (the Italian for shield) to a new 911 model that featured a novel detachable roof panel. It is now standard terminology for the system, although a Porsche-registered trademark.
Telematics	Any individual communication to a car from an outside base station, for example, satellite navigation signals, automatic emergency calls, roadside assistance, traffic information and dynamic route guidance.
Transaxle	Engineering shorthand for 'transmission axle': this is the clutch and gearbox unit that is connected to the driveshafts to transfer power to the driven wheels. All front-wheel-drive and rear- or mid-engined, rear-wheel-drive cars have some type of transaxle.

Where the New Models were Launched

Barcelona International Motor Show
26 April –
4 May 2003

Concept

Alfa Romeo 8C
  Competizione
Lancia Granturismo
  Stilnovo
Seat Cupra GT

Frankfurt Motor Show
13–21 September 2003

Concept

Audi Le Mans
Citroën C-Airlounge
Daihatsu ai
Ford Visos
Jaguar R-D6
Lancia Fulvia Coupé
Mazda Kusabi
Mitsubishi i
Nissan Dunehawk
Opel Insignia
Peugeot 407 Elixir
Renault BeBop
Saab 9-3
  Sport-Hatch
Skoda Roomster
Suzuki Concept S2
Toyota CS&S
Volkswagen
  Concept R

Production

Aston Martin DB9
BMW 5 Series
BMW 6 Series
BMW X3
Citroën C2
Daewoo Lacetti
Fiat Panda

Kia Picanto
Maserati Quattroporte
Mazda3
Mercedes-Benz SLR
  McLaren
Mitsubishi Grandis
Opel/Vauxhall Astra
Smart Forfour
Subaru Justy
Subaru Legacy
  and Outback
Volkswagen Golf

Tokyo Motor Show
25 October –
5 November 2003

Concept

Daihatsu UFE-II
Honda HSC
Honda IMAS
Honda Kiwami
Hyundai Neos-II
Jeep Treo
Lexus LF-S and LF-X
Mazda Ibuki
Mercedes-Benz F500
  Mind
Mitsubishi Se-ro
Nissan Conran Cube
Nissan Effis
Nissan Fuga
Nissan Jikoo
Nissan Redigo
Nissan Serenity
Subaru B9 Scrambler
Subaru R1e
Suzuki Landbreeze
Suzuki Mobile Terrace
Suzuki S-Ride
Toyota NLSV
Toyota PM

Production

Honda Odyssey
Subaru R2

Greater LA Auto Show
4–12 January 2004

Concept

Hummer H3T

Production

Chevrolet Cobalt
Saab 9-2X

North American International Auto Show (NAIAS)
Detroit
10–19 January 2004

Concept

Chevrolet Nomad
Chrysler ME
  Four-Twelve
Dodge Sling Shot
Ford Bronco
Honda SUT
Hyundai HCD8
Jeep Rescue
Land Rover Range
  Stormer
Lincoln Aviator
Lincoln Mark X
Mazda MX-Micro
  Sport
Mercedes-Benz
  Vision GST
Mitsubishi Eclipse
  Concept-E
Mitsubishi Sport Truck
Nissan Actic
Saturn Curve
Toyota FTX
Volkswagen
  Concept T

Production

Chevrolet Corvette
Ford Five Hundred
Ford Freestyle
Ford Mustang
Infiniti QX56
Kia Spectra
Lexus GS
Nissan Frontier
Nissan Pathfinder
Pontiac G6
Pontiac Solstice
Scion tC
Volvo S40 and V50

Melbourne International Motor Show
27 February –
8 March 2004

Concept

Joss

Production

Elfin MS8

Brussels International Motor Show
15–25 January 2004

Concept

Renault Trafic
  Deck'up

Canadian International Auto Show
13–22 February 2004

Production

Chrysler 300C

74th Geneva International Motor Show
4–14 March 2004

Concept

EDAG genX
Fiat Trepiuno
Fioravanti Kite
Fuore BlackJag
Hyundai E3
Italdesign Alfa Romeo
  Visconti
Italdesign Toyota
  Alessandro Volta
Mazda MX-Flexa
Nissan Qashqai
Opel Trixx
Renault Modus
Renault Wind
Rinspeed Splash
Rolls-Royce 100EX
Toyota MTRC
Volkswagen
  Concept C
Volvo YCC

Production

Audi A6
Lancia Musa
Mercedes-Benz CLS
  Coupé
Mercedes-Benz SLK
Mitsubishi Colt
Peugeot 407
Seat Altea
Skoda Octavia
Toyota Corolla Verso

Paris Motor Show (Mondial de l'automobile)
25 September – 10 October 2004
Paris Expo, Paris, France
www.mondialauto.tm.fr

Tokyo Motor Show
3–7 November 2004
Nippon Convention Centre, Chiba City, Tokyo
www.tokyo-motorshow.com

Greater LA Auto Show
7–16 January 2005
Los Angeles Convention Center, Los Angeles, USA
www.laautoshow.com

North American International Auto Show (NAIAS)
15–23 January 2005
Cobo Center, Detroit, USA
www.naias.com

Chicago Auto Show
11–20 February 2005
McCormick Place South, Chicago, USA
www.chicagoautoshow.com

Canadian International Auto Show
18–27 February 2005
Metro Toronto Convention Centre and SkyDome, Toronto, Canada
www.autoshow.ca

75th Geneva International Motor Show
3–13 March 2005
Palexpo, Geneva, Switzerland
www.salon-auto.ch

Melbourne International Motor Show
4–14 March 2005
Melbourne Exhibition Centre, Melbourne, Australia
www.motorshow.com.au

New York International Auto Show
9–18 April 2005
Jacob Javits Convention Center, New York, USA
www.autoshowny.com

Frankfurt Motor Show
15–25 September 2005
Trade Fairgrounds, Frankfurt am Main, Germany
www.iaa.de

Marques and their Parent Companies

Hundreds of separate car-making companies have consolidated over the past decade into ten groups: General Motors, Ford, DaimlerChrysler, VW, Toyota, Peugeot, Renault, BMW, Honda and Hyundai. These account for at least nine of every ten cars produced globally today. The remaining independent marques either produce specialist models, offer niche design and engineering services or tend to be at risk because of their lack of economies of scale. The global over-capacity in the industry means that manufacturers are having to offer increased choice to the consumer to differentiate their brands and maintain market share.

BMW
BMW
Mini
Riley*
Rolls-Royce
Triumph*

DaimlerChrysler
Chrysler
De Soto*
Dodge
Hudson*
Imperial*
Jeep
Maybach
Mercedes-Benz
Mitsubishi
Nash*
Plymouth*
Smart

Fiat Auto
Abarth*
Alfa Romeo
Autobianchi*
Ferrari
Fiat
Innocenti*
Lancia
Maserati

Ford
Aston Martin
Daimler*
Ford
Jaguar
Lagonda*
Land Rover
Lincoln
Mazda
Mercury
Range Rover
Volvo

General Motors
Buick
Cadillac
Chevrolet
Daewoo
GMC
Holden
Hummer
Isuzu
Oldsmobile*
Opel
Pontiac
Saab
Saturn
Subaru
Suzuki
Vauxhall

Honda
Acura
Honda

Hyundai
Asia Motors
Hyundai
Kia

MG Rover
Austin*
MG
Morris*
Rover
Wolseley*

Peugeot
Citroën
Hillman*
Humber*
Panhard*
Peugeot
Simca*
Singer*
Sunbeam*
Talbot*

Proton
Lotus
Proton

Renault
Alpine*
Dacia
Datsun*
Infiniti
Nissan
Renault
Renault Sport

Toyota
Daihatsu
Lexus
Scion
Toyota

VW
Audi
Auto Union*
Bentley
Bugatti
Cosworth
DKW*
Horch*
Lamborghini
NSU*
Seat
Skoda
Volkswagen
Wanderer*

Independent marques
Austin-Healey*
Bertone
Bristol
Caterham
EDAG
Elfin
Fioravanti
Heuliez
Invicta
Irmscher
Italdesign
Jensen
Joss
Koenigsegg
Lada
Mitsuoka
Morgan
Pininfarina
Porsche
Rinspeed
Sivax
SsangYong
Tata
TVR
Venturi
Westfield
Zagato

* Dormant marques

Acknowledgements

I should first like to thank everyone at Merrell Publishers who has helped to ensure that the *Car Design Yearbook* series has been thoroughly established as the annual guide to new car design across the world. I should especially like to thank Anthea Snow, Nicola Bailey, Michelle Draycott and Kirsty Seymour-Ure.

Thanks are also due to the manufacturers' press offices, who have been particularly supportive during the creation of this edition in their supply of photographic and technical material. I should like to thank Hannah James-Roll and S-D for their encouragement, Giles Chapman for his professional editorial support, and Alistair Layzell for his continued success with the public relations campaign.

Stephen Newbury
Henley-on-Thames, Oxfordshire
2004

Picture Credits